Flock & Shadow

new and
selected poems

The publication of *Flock and Shadow: New and Selected Poems* is made possible by the generous support of the McKnight Foundation and other contributors to New Rivers Press.

For academic permission please contact Frederick T. Courtright at 570.839.7477 or permdude@eclipse.net. For all other permissions, contact The Copyright Clearance Center at 978.750.8400 or info@copyright.com.

New Rivers Press is a nonprofit literary press associated with Minnesota State University Moorhead.

Wayne Gudmundson, Director
Alan Davis, Senior Editor
Thom Tammaro, Poetry Editor
Donna Carlson, Managing Editor
        Honors Apprentice: Rosanne Pfenning
        Flock and Shadow: New and Selected Poems book team: Diana
            Goble and Amber Langford
        Editorial interns: Fauntel DeShayes, Tessa Dietz, Kacy Friddle,
            Diana Goble, Jill Haugen, Amber Langford, Jens Larson,
            Samantha Miller, Kurt Olerud, Tamera Parrish, Heather
            Steinmann, Melissa Sumas, Abbey Thompsen
        Design interns: Katie Elenberger, Allison Garske, Amanda
            Ketterling, Jocie Salveson, Lindsay Staber, Amy Wilcox
        Communications Coordinator: Gerri Stowman and Teresa Schafer
        Literary Festival Coordinator: Jill Haugen
        Fundraising Coordinator: Jens Larson
        Website Coordinator: Conor Shenk
Marlane Sanderson and Deb Hval, Business Manager
Allen Sheets, Design Manager
Nancy E. Hanson, Events Manager
Liz Conmey, Marketing Manager

Printed in the United States of America.

New Rivers Press
c/o MSUM
1104 7th Avenue South
Moorhead, MN 56563
www.newriverspress.com

The wonder of the world,
The beauty and the power,
The shapes of things,
Their colors, lights, and shades;
These I saw.
Look ye also, while life lasts.
        —inscription on a gravestone
          in Cumberland, England

It's only men and women who long
for a lost unity....
        —John Berger, *Photocopies*

For Colleen, Matthew, and Caitlin Hettich

Table of Contents

1

New Poems

Some Days Just Feel Like

the book I continue intending to read
or the rhythm I blink with my eyes, or the moons
in my fingernails as I scratch your back
and look out the window beyond you, into

a wilderness of bushes we planted just a year ago,
now filled with purple berries and lizards
the length of my finger; the guide book full
of useful lies, like the color of the lake

we intend some day to live beside
or the river that flows beneath our house
full of transparent fish we eat
sometimes when we curl around each other

too tightly to sleep, or wake in an unfamiliar
outskirt of our lives, where the accents are leafy
and windblown and full of useless gestures
like free improvisations without

melody, stories that flesh no plot,
or books we could intend to read
for years—until our lives are separate
from our bodies, and we are everywhere.

Visiting Hour

A man painted blue would visit my bedroom
when I lived behind the pine trees, nestled in that small hill,
inside that little house filled with de-clawed cats
whose coats smelled of perfume. Like your hair.
He lived in a blue room just behind my eyes,
in front of my brain's brain, and when he visited
I stayed in bed and let him stroke my hair
until that feeling was inside me again,
that feeling that there's always the possibility of gentleness,
that feeling of pleasure where the hair meets the scalp,
where the skin meets the body, where the world meets again,
behind which the blue man lived. You know
I never had a father but the man who went to work
and I never had a mother but the woman who gave birth
to me and then to me and then to me and me again.
I mean they could never explain why the trees
asked riddles of each other but wouldn't tell me anything
except when the wind blew. Sometimes other colors
unfolded from my body, in different forms: a red fox
and many white birds, deer, a school of too-bright
phosphorescent minnows, even mushrooms in a dark wood
deeper in the forest. But the blue man spoke a language
I knew, which was *window* and *deep sky* and *sleep*,
think-of-me-fondly and *you're not alone*
alone, while those parents I'd never met called me
and the room I was sitting in filled with snow.

Romance

She talked about the faces we've memorized so well
we no longer see them. She looked at me, squinting,
and wondered which self might be irrelevant
in this colorized landscape, where birds fly in no clear
pattern, like feelings. And doesn't the sky pale
each time we look up, and every time we mention blue?
So I imagine caves, she said, and so I breathe
cool air as we walk down into dripping earth,
wondering how deep we must go before there's only dark,
before we've vanished. Could we understand our bodies
well enough to see, could we wake the senses
we've never even thought about, to light our way down
where creatures have no use for eyes,
down where creatures are more pale than air,
down where we might even make our own light
and see? So why not practice breathing
with our bodies, until we can swim as far down
as we might desire, hollow out our thoughts
until we are light enough to fly, unfold
our wings like black umbrellas, and flap
unselfconsciously, thinking sky or wind,
the self that is all self, make an adequate
language from the center of everything, and sing?

Specialist

He said he could hear what people were saying
in cars on the highway
even when they were blasting their radios.

He told me he could recognize my heart beat
as soon as I walked into his office, even
while I was sitting in the waiting room and he was
treating a patient much sicker than I.

He said he could hear the unexplored terrain inside:
huge fields no human had visited, with birds
rising just above the tall grass,

gliding there, landing, singing in patterns
that always sounded new, and in harmony. He scowled
as he stared off into space, then told me the woods
on the other side of that field were full

of owls the size of our children when they're learning
to talk, which is huge for a raptor. Then he smiled
and opened his arms for a hug, so he could

feel those secrets I still couldn't tell
and sense which flowers would heal me.

Work

On the ride home I'd furtively watch this woman
we called China Doll, with stick-skinny legs
and skimpy plastic skirt, huge cone-shaped breasts
that seemed transposed from another person's body,
a white-powdered face and black-banged wig,
who sat at the back of the smoking car and smiled
crookedly at the strangers who sat down beside her
for a kiss and a caress. I watched her follow
a man off the train once, one of those who'd kissed her—
a young man in a camelhair coat—and walk
beside him in her high heels, across
the dusting of fresh snow on the ice that had been there
so long it had turned black, and reach out to rest
her bare hand—the afternoon was freezing—across
his shoulder so she wouldn't slip and fall. He brushed it
away with his glove and sauntered toward
the parking lot. She followed. The train was crowded
so it lingered in the station, long enough for me
to watch him open the passenger door
of his wood-paneled station wagon. He left it hanging open,
walked quickly around to the driver's side,
got in and closed the door. And then he started up—
I could see the plume of gray smoke spewing an impatient cloud.
But she had slipped and fallen on the black ice at the curb
and was just then brushing herself off, standing
straight again, walking with a wobble to his car,
taking tiny half steps, her sexy wig askew.

Interior

Knives were talking in that stuffy room
built into the softest parts of the body,
where the light is always a buttery yellow
and the day outside seems a lifetime away.
They talked of love. And so of course they lied.

When my children were young, one of these knives
said, *I used to climb with them*
high into our oak tree and tell them they could fly,
which they knew they couldn't do.

And then I'd tell them I could fly too
and let myself fall from the tree, and try
to land like a stab in the dirt, and call them
to somersault and fall. All those other knives

whisper and laugh. They gleam their applause
in that yellow light, as the hot house flowers
in the vase by the window that looks out on nothing
but vital innards start to sing
of scattered seed, of bees and sky.

The cat curled up on the counter purrs.
A mouse without a tail runs across the bloody floor.

Wash

These are the days you forget about feeling
while you impart morals and syntax, and how
to bait a fish hook with anything at all
and catch that rare species that has no bones
to speak of, which lies so passively there
in the bucket, like a rubber glove.

Your children never look at you.
They pretend you are their dog or goldfish or hamster
or wide-screen TV.
They examine your wrinkles and life lines
and pronounce you stale. Nothing will oblige.

Your husband is a tennis racket minus the strings.
Your husband is a baseball mitt wrapped in rubber bands.
Your husband is an empty wetsuit stored beneath the bed
when your children carry nightmares like broken dolls
in to sleep between you. The rules are as follows:

No singing in the shower or off color jokes
and please don't stay naked any longer than you must.
Don't let the water run, and please don't flush
every time you take a leak. Never mention you know what.

You must ask permission. Say please. Use soap
every time you touch another person or yourself
or anything at all. You've probably been told
soap is made from fat, boiled down and mixed
with perfume and ash. Don't think about it. Wash.

Attributes of Love

Here we see a man with too many arms
to control what he reaches for.
Here we see someone whose body is so numb
he never stops talking to taste anyone.
And here we have a man who was born without ears,
who listens with his profile. He can hear whispers
across vast fields, even what you haven't
said yet, what you never will.
This man wants to be a baseball, so he can
fly, and this man thinks if he could
photocopy silence he'd be content as air.
Now look more closely: Here we have a woman
who has pulled out her bones. She breast feeds the air.
This woman paints herself with tattoos of veins,
and she wants to make love until she is fluent
in French or Japanese, so she can travel
anywhere, without being seen.

Their children are paper, which is made from trees
and bits of cloth, from grass. Pressed flat.
Their children are glass, which is made from sand
and heat. Their children drive fast, act wild.

Sweat

My first girl's mother exercised
by walking up and down the stairs
of their elegant house, from attic to basement
and back. For hours. She wore a jogging suit
and she listened to soap operas on the TVs
she blared from each floor. Sometimes she called out
to the characters, panting. Then she'd rest
in the kitchen with a small glass of juice and talk
on the phone, sighing, still breathing
with gusto, patting her forehead with a damp cloth
and proudly stretching her legs.

Her daughter took bubble baths while I sat
in the hallway outside her bathroom door
and played folk songs on guitar, leaning
toward the keyhole, so she could hear me
over those soap opera voices.
Eventually she'd emerge, wrapped in a huge towel,
and slip past, into her bedroom to dress.
Of course I was eager to see her new outfits,
to smell her perfumes and lotions and oils—

so I claimed I was writing love songs, out there
in the hallway, and I played what snippets of tunes
I could imagine, from records I hoped she'd never heard,
with such simple chords my clumsy fingers
eventually sounded graceful, even
musical enough to charm her into
the love I imagined so vividly
my singing grew strangled, into a kind of howl.

Sleep

Now she could relax. With the kitchen finally clean
and her husband asleep in front of the TV,
the children long gone to bed and everything
mundane accounted for, she could put on
her ear phones and listen to the music she loved most,
Mahler's Fourth Symphony, and imagine another
life. She could feel it so vividly she seemed
to float away into sound, to become someone else
entirely, with memories, joys, dreams:
At her kitchen table in her bathrobe, with the lights
still blazing, she walked by a rain-scented river
on a cool spring morning, a young girl with a crush
on a stranger and a love of rain and rivers
like this, and rocks, especially rocks
that glinted with mica. She loved to stand
at the railing and look out at the swallows while flowers
bloomed across the hill behind her.
In the distance a train whistled. Someone was singing.
She turned as though dancing to a folk song, in German,
and felt light enough to blow away and had to stop herself
before she was transposed. In the living room, her husband
stirred and growled: His marriage had become
an arrangement, a distant friendship at best,
much worse at worst. The TV was tuned
to a cop show, was tuned to the news: celebrities
and small scale catastrophes. He would remember

no trace of his dreams unless his wife woke him
on her way upstairs, still humming.
But sometimes she forgot him and he slept there, bathed
in the TV's blather, while directly above,
his children lay tucked into their beds like the sweet little
mammals they still were, whose breath smelled of rain.

Spell

While my uncle the chemist mixed concoctions
in the basement, I sat on the plastic-covered couch
beside my grandfather, who chain smoked while he read aloud
from *Grimm's Fairy Tales* and precariously balanced
a full ashtray on the knob of his knee.
Deep in her recliner, grandmother knitted sweaters
for the refugees. She hummed as she sewed—
always a tune which made me feel sleepy.
But then another slow train passed, rattling
the windows, and my uncle in a stained white tee shirt
came upstairs, talking gleefully,
incomprehensibly, about some great discoveries
he would make someday. We'd take a walk together
to try out a new slingshot, or a rocket he'd invented,
to the scrubby lot scattered with broken test tubes,
burned cans, pools of oily muck.
He'd make a fire and talk about hypotheses and plans—
things I couldn't understand.
When the streetlights came on, he'd sometimes talk
about love, as we held hands and walked home through the dark,
about women he watched from a distance,
how they talked and laughed and ignored him, how
his inventions would make someone happy, someday.

The Father

Yesterday my daughter came home
carrying a wing she had fashioned in art class—
as tall as I am, which is not very tall
for a person but huge for a wing—built
of wire and wax paper that looked like skin,
and hair she'd cut from her classmates' heads
and glued down. No feathers. *That was one of the rules,*
she told me, *we have to make wings without feathers,*
that strap onto our arms. Then we're supposed to fly,
or pretend to, while our friends imagine birds
and draw us way up there. And then we'll draw them too.
When I tapped the wing lightly it sounded like a drum.
It's beautiful, I told her, and then I went inside
while she strapped the wing on and started running around
the yard, lopsided for a bird: One wing
only makes a person fall over.
So I helped her build a second wing, but it didn't match,
which was all right by me, since I didn't really want her
flying anyway, at least not without
protection: a parachute, or a net to break her fall.
I helped her fail, though both her wings are beautiful.
Maybe they are beautiful *because* they don't quite match,
I suggested over dinner, unconvinced myself.
She scowled. And then she smiled. Later we went out—
after the dew had fallen—and tried
to lift spider webs from the trees without

spoiling their symmetry. *These will staunch a wound*
better than a Band-Aid, or a cotton ball, she said
as dusk fell around us, like fragrance or a breeze.
I wanted to ask her *what wound do you mean?*
as though I might staunch it myself, but she was
holding a web suspended in her hands,
like air, or like nothing, and passing it to me.

Forgiveness

We could wade from that island into clear ocean
for hundreds of yards before the water
was even up to our knees.
We could sit there and watch small birds, and vultures
so high they hardly seemed to move.
We could walk out even further, to where the sand dropped off,
where the water was dark and muscular—
and we could push ourselves out into that dark deep
full of the ghosts of huge fish we feared
were fished out now, even while we shivered
with the fear of being watched from below.
We could reach a sand bar, almost out of sight.
We could stay out until dusk and swim back through the dark.
Or rain could start to fall, so hard we couldn't hear
each other, or ourselves. And sea birds—gulls and pelicans,
cormorants, terns, anhingas—could float
to that sand bar to wait out the rain. They could be
close enough to touch, all around us. And when the rain
stopped abruptly, they could take off
in a burst, all directions. The water could feel cold
as we swam back, and the surface we swam through
could be fresh enough to drink. And it could smell of flowers.

Sky Full of White Birds

1.

On windy days, seagulls huddled on the windowsills outside my parents' bedroom. I'd stand by the window and watch them and wonder at my skin and heavy body, while my parents moved around downstairs with the radio news turned low. My father's shoes in the closet smelled like living animals, and I thought about sweat. And then I decided to stand very still, until my hearing vanished and my eyes grew skin. By the time my mother called me down to dinner I'd have vanished for a little while. I wanted to tell them how it felt to disappear. Instead we talked about those huge nets fishermen throw from their boats, nets that open for miles and strain the ocean bare of living things.

Mushrooms grew overnight, all over the back yard. Sailboat masts clanged in the harbor, where we once saw a seal, where we often saw dead fish and condoms and trash. Boys my age would catch horseshoe crabs just to turn them upside down and watch them slowly die. Boys I was friends with caught nets of minnows they spilled out onto the dock, just to throw knives into their bodies, just to see how long they would flip-flop after they'd been cut in half.

The seagulls hovered overhead, with other birds I still can't name.

2.

Then I was a small boy high up in a winter tree, afraid to come down. There were alley cats above me, prowling and yowling, and I wondered where my friends had gone, who'd climbed so much faster and higher, laughing down at me. There were pieces of cloth in the tree's twiggy branches. Down below, frozen puddles and the ashes of a leaf fire. And then my friends, standing on the ground, were laughing up at me. And I was laughing too, though I was freezing and afraid to move.

Dead swan by the water's edge, huge and filled with seaweed.
Dead swan by the water's edge, big enough to climb inside...

I slept on a beach, out in the open, under a towel, covered in sand. In the middle of the night large creatures pulled themselves from the ocean and settled down near me.

Birds flew all night there. I slept by listening.

The soul is a circle, someone had told me, when I was young and impressionable. So I tried to imagine what such a circle looked like. I knew something inside me was clear like spring water yet grained like wood and fragrant like pine woods early summer mornings. I knew something inside me was happy and clear and would always be that way, no matter what else happened.

And if we came across the vivid breath, blowing through an ordinary landscape, would we stand still and inhale, or would we walk on, safe in our smaller selves, free of that feeling that takes us beyond and leaves us abandoned, out of breath and hungry. Like a stone no one picks up to build with or to throw.

Underneath that stone, thousands of insects, some of which no scientist has named, are building deep houses and secret tunnels underground.

3.

I walked all day, pulling through the branches, each of which was dotted with pussy willow cotton balls which turned, as I walked further, into pieces of cloth caught on thorns all around me, and ashes that had fallen from some huge distant fire. There were small forest birds flitting here and there. The ground was sandy and covered with sharp leaves.

Then someone said he remembered when the wind had blown backward, and when it had blown without moving.

And then someone else, who knew all the stories about wind, told us how it grew hair and barked, how it blew down your house, how it made things wear away, including its own body, way back when the world was solid and new.

And I can only tell you more than I know because I am a student of rhythms and breath, because I am a student of gestures and blinking, because I am a student of the guts and groans of horses in glittering fields, of small birds flying through tall grass without brushing a single blade. Then landing there, safely hidden, to sing.

The Simple Man

*I am at home here, in the dream where the sky
and the ground come together under my skin
and run through me like blood.*
                    –Elaine Neil Orr

The simple man lived in a single room in a mostly abandoned part of the city. He woke early every day and walked, talking to everyone—though few replied—and collecting interesting junk which he carried a few blocks or miles and put down, to pick up something else—another piece of interesting junk, which he carried awhile and abandoned as well. And so he spent his days walking and collecting things, moving things around. By the time he got home in the evening he was usually empty-handed and content. He had no other work and he had no friends. What money he had—and he didn't have much—came from a job he'd held many years before, when he wasn't quite so simple. At night he ate soup from a can, and then he sat in his favorite chair and started counting out loud, as high as he could before he fell asleep, as dusk or night filled the room

and sometimes the musician who lived upstairs would hear him counting as he climbed to his apartment, carrying his nightly bag of groceries, happy to be home so he could practice the tunes he'd been thinking all day. The simple man's door was always half open, even in this run-down, funky neighborhood, and the musician could hear the counting, which always made him think of some fundamental rhythm he'd like to try someday, that went on and on like air goes in our lungs and out and in, out and in, on and on. He'd unlock the dozen locks on his door, open the kitchen window for the air and start cooking elaborate one-man dinners, with bebop on the stereo. Then he'd pick up his instrument and start to play, scales for the first half-hour, then chords and melodies, and finally improvisations late into the night

which no one else but the simple man heard through his counting, though the musician dreamed women were listening, the women he admired as he walked around carrying dresses and flowers and desserts all day, all over the city, invisible in his work as any man can be. He never took the subway because it hurt his ears, so he walked many miles, watching things and thinking music. And then one day there was this one girl—

he called her a girl though she was really a woman—who'd heard him play on the street once, at Bryant Park, mid-afternoon one quiet Saturday, who'd stayed a long time watching him, watching his fingers and the way he moved his hands up and down the neck of his instrument, the way he leaned into the melody he played. She'd put a ten-dollar bill into the hat, along with a scrawled phone number which he hadn't had the nerve to call for a week at least or maybe two—and then when he had called a gruff male voice had barked *yeah what*—and he hadn't known her name, so he couldn't ask for anything, so he only said *excuse me*

and hung up. Saturday he carries his guitar from corner to corner—for money, sure, but mostly to hear how he sounds in the air, to see if he can stop people for a moment. He never talks to anyone, really, not in the way he wishes he could. And he never plays in clubs. He's never had a band. Sometimes at night he plays along with bebop records—always bebop, though he has a much more mellow style, quiet, a style that charmed her, that woman he often thinks about, who lives somewhere else, who was only visiting the family she feels mostly estranged from, who happened to be walking to the library that morning she saw him, who fell in love with him a little just seeing him play, who sometimes feels the need to suffer for love, who takes the train now across miles of suburbs to Grand Central Station, gets out and walks on 42nd street to where she saw him, then sits in the park

and waits. She is so beautiful, man after man can't walk by without sitting down to look at her. The brave ones ask if they can buy her a drink. But she says no, she's waiting for someone. Of course. And as she sits there surrounded by pigeons and suitors the simple man walks by carrying a suitcase he found outside Penn Station that morning. He kneels on the bright green grass and opens the suitcase to free a small kitten which runs away from him, toward the pigeons which burst up a moment, then land unafraid. The young woman is indignant when she sees the simple man walk quickly away, leaving that kitten to fend for itself, chased now by a little girl in a pink party dress whose mother says *no* and *no* and *yes, I guess so. It looks clean*

enough. The woman follows the simple man home, through winding streets and dark alleys—she doesn't know quite why. And when she gets to his apartment she follows him upstairs to see where this strange man lives, what he does there. After all, she's studying to be a journalist or a social worker or a psychologist at her college. As she climbs up the stairs after the simple man, calling *hello hello hello* behind him the love of her life bounds down the stairs toward her, instrument in hand, whistling bebop, thinking chord progressions and melodies. They pass each other without recognition, like breath and wind. It will be years before they meet again.

Thread

–after a photograph
in The New York Times

A man on a hunger strike sews his own lips
and eyelids together, with thick black thread,
with heavy thread meant for sewing winter clothes,
jackets and knit caps to keep the ears warm.
He sits in some corner and starves for his asylum.

I sit at my dining room table and study
his face in the newspaper photograph: at first glance
he looks like an extremely fashionable pierced
hipster, sutures jagged through his thin lips,
long eyelashes almost hiding the raw
thread he sewed there. His lips are slightly
parted, as far as they will open,
and he seems to be trying to speak. In fact
he seems to be singing, eyes sewed tight—

songs so potent he could wind up in jail
back home for just whispering
one of their refrains.

2

from
Looking Out (1982),
Lathe (1987), and
A Small Boat (1990)

Bees

Where I was born
bees were believed
to cause silence, neighborhood
boundaries were drawn
in accent and hive.
I grew up slowly
where there were too many
flowers and too few
stars, where nightly
a cloud seeped through
the window and hung
above my mother's sleeping head.

She is reading, half asleep,
and does not notice me
enter the room. I speak her name,
she does not answer. When I
reach out
to touch her
she bursts into flowers
like speech after years
of silence. I think
I know now how bees
make silence.
I know why they sting.
I gather my mother.

Miracle Cure

When I heard my father was becoming a great grizzly bear,
I was stunned for a moment, of course, and not
completely relieved, as I am now.
Mother called so late I thought it was the cancer.
I had already panicked and packed so I could drop everything
and fly home to console her. Miracle of medicine!
But will he grow taller? Will he smell? And he'll have
a temper. We'll have to move into the country,
she said, because of his temper and smell,
and I'm nervous out there in the country—all those
domestic animals
and wild nights full of stars,
and friendly people in hats. Bring a hat,
please, when you come. Thank you. They dried up
his cancer the only way they could, and I'm thankful,
she said, although he'll soon forget
who I am, will remember only his hunger,
will be a grizzly bear. Bring tools.
We'll build his cage together.
We'll build him a fine home out there in the country.
We'll learn to adjust. He'll probably outlive us all!

Your Mother Sings

Your mother sings
an old song as she
hangs the wash. She looks around—

And when she is sure
no one is watching
(but you are watching) she lets the pigeons

she keeps at the bottom of her laundry basket
fly free—
Each has a note

in its beak. And now a pigeon
flies in your window, dies at your feet.
The note says: *I live alone, please*

come, please help me. But she doesn't live
alone, your mother
is downstairs now

moving pots and pans, starting
dinner, singing
a song she sang,

you imagine, when you couldn't sleep.
You hear her down there
singing. You see the pigeon on the floor.

You Have Lived

You have lived in a place where you could watch horses
walk to the edge of the surf and stand biting
wave foam, swishing their tails, until
shore birds you never noticed in the air
lighted on their backs
and started pecking there.

Then the horses reared into waves. And you
squinted, riding them, child then, turning
pink in the sun. And you remember them often,
squinting at the grease-spattered pelicans you love,
who patrol this turquoise,
this south. You've seen

a pelican flying up the beach with his lower beak
torn away, fishing line trailing down
into the water to skim along
the water. You've watched him. You've dreamed you could
          nurse him
back to his health. Yes, you could feed him
from your closets: shoe-fish, clutter, rags.

You could give him a name. But the bird flies calmly,
as though nothing at all were wrong, glancing
into the water for fish, moving
up and down the beach that is crowded
with junk and people, strangers who look,
you realize suddenly,
exactly like you.

Romance

Your father kneels on the roof, cleaning
gutters while your mother
types letters to magazines
thanking them, and you
walk around
your bedroom, doors closed, humming all
afternoon, identifying
birds in your head, in your shadows on the wall.

The woman you'll marry is talking politics,
hunger, the war that is not quite
happening all
over the world
and the ones that are killing nobody
you've ever known, but you haven't met her yet.
She lives down the street. You won't touch her for years.

Summer Rain

Today you drifted away as though
our bed were the dock I saw a man dive off
once and swim without looking back
far out, into the current's
propellers and swirl.

                                Because I was looking
across the channel at the jets rising
like nonsense from behind the apartments I didn't
notice until
he was beyond help, and by
the time I'd called out he'd become indistinct—

and I thought: Why gesture and look like a fool,
they'll never find any trace. So I stared
hard at the buildings, the jets and the boats,
and as I did so his image grew clearer.
I remembered how he'd undressed before jumping in,
how he'd folded his clothes; there were his clothes:
suit, shirt, tie folded neatly
on the bench beside me; and as I felt

the material, still
staring out,
I remembered the tune he'd sung under
his breath. We've sung it. I remembered a name,
a family, bits of a childhood, so
I took off my old clothes, changed into his
and thought of the shade your eyes would turn, deep blue,
when you saw me in a new suit
as I walked home through the summer rain.

First Love

In winter my father and I would drive
a shortcut from town across the lake.
We'd zoom, stamp the brakes and feel ourselves
sail. We'd laugh, knowing how wide
and thick the ice was, how few people
there'd be all winter. We'd do it again
and again until we reached
our shore.

Clear days I'd walk out, cut a hole
to fish through. Sometimes I'd lie face down
over the hole, look into my own eyes
and taste the cold.

One day I heard a car.

Looked up to see my father speeding,
spinning across the cloudy ice.
I pulled my line in, stood there smiling,
holding a fish,
when I understood
as though the ice had broken beneath me,
I understood the car was spinning
out of control, was sailing to take
my breath. And then I dreamed: I watched

the hole growing fast as my father spun
toward me. My father would plunge instead
and sink. I would have the choice
of saving my father or taking his place.

I'd never loved him so perfectly, standing there
waiting for him to sink completely,
then diving. The water
was too cold to swim in.
My teeth are still white
and the moons in my thumbs
are still frozen. They will never melt.

By spring we'd moved south.

Calmly While the Roof Swells

Somewhere in a back room we're not even sure
exists in our house, the old people waiting
for us to grow old too and wear them hang
like wallpaper, peeling, or dry-cleaned suits,
and although we never
open the door
to look in, and although we're not quite sure
there *is* a door, they murmur like the ceilings
in old houses do when it rains and the wood
swells to keep us dry: We listen

and hear the hairs inside that can't
find pores to push through
push and curl
back, a nest of hair inside.
And we hear the birds that circle within
and without for the choice nest-stuff to lay in,
and we sit talking calmly while the roof
swells and our grandparents murmur, we hardly
remember them now, their waiting through the walls.

Almost Out of Sight

You walk dead-low tide sand bars, collecting
shells, making flocks run, fly up, land,
to peck at the sand, to fly up again.

Out here, the faint line of shore matters less
than the least shell you hold, is less alive
than the minnows that nibble your ankles. You wade in,
arms held up, as if what you carried
would melt, thinking
of your grandfather, who turned,
he said, as far out of sight as you are now,

into a huge
swordfish he called it,
and ate himself up, and spat himself out,
then traveled the wide world under, to be caught,
he said, by a beer-bellied cowboy in a distant land
who didn't even have
the decency to eat him.

—Stuffed and hung him on a wall in a cluttered
air-conditioned condo in a big foreign city.
Impressed all his friends with his monster, your grand
father, who had traveled the wide world and been
a millionaire over and over, who told you

how it felt
to breathe underwater,
how the shells had danced at twilight,
throwing their skirts up
as he swam by, hungry and sleek, and real—.

Shells for your teeth,
the color of your eyes.

I Remember When

my father climbed the western mountain.
Every day he chopped more
of its peak off so we could have more
daylight to grow our food in, and when he'd
chopped deep enough that in midsummer we had
sun for an extra minute, which
is, of course, an exaggeration, he
knew he had done something real, and called us
to watch the sun settle
in the chink and disappear.

Next day the sun had moved, but he kept digging
the same dent, wanting one day a year.
One day, he told us, the mountain would be
chopped in two and there would be
one complete day
hours longer than there'd ever been.

People in the town called him "Father" too.
Some volunteered to help, but no,
it was his, his dent and his light; they were lucky
he was willing to share. At night there were new stars.

—When he hit a spring and the water gushed out
a waterfall, flooding the valley and the town,
to form a beautiful lake, deep,
cold, and full of fish found
nowhere else, the animals that lived
wild on his mountain rejoiced and grew
wilder, more passionate. They rejoiced!
We still do.

Down at the Docks

You find yourself rolling loaded dice in an old boat, down in the cave where the crewmen sleep. Fish seem to swim in the air around you, attracted, you imagine, to your voice. They dart away at the sharp sound of the dice and hang as shadows, part of the darkness. The men pretend to pay you what they owe, and then they pretend to go to sleep.

She was buying a flank of fish when you emerged from below decks, black suit and dark glasses slightly steamed, pockets bulging. Her hair was on fire. The fish she was pointing to still flapped on the dock. It had to be fresh, you heard her explain, she was having the man she had decided to love as no other to dinner for the first time, tonight. You whispered to your sleeve, but for the first time in your life, he didn't reply.

Sailors were swimming around the boat now, diving down for the coins you threw into the water to impress her, but she never so much as glanced your way.

Her fillets squirmed in their wrapping, in her purse, as she walked up the dock and disappeared. Lost in your loneliness, you never noticed as the boat you were standing on started slowly to burn, down in its belly, where you had won the pebbles you now flicked into the harbor, one by one. Smoke started rising through the deck, and when the sailors and fish pushed the boat into the current, fish of fire were leaping from the floor.

You have forgotten how to swim. You are reluctant to take off your clothes lest she smell the smoke, turn and see your naked body, such an unimpressive sight. There is something you like about this hopeless situation. You decide, finally, simply to burn.

Colorado

–for Colleen

High above trees,
still climbing, your eyes
turned so blue
the lake we leaned
to drink from had no
bottom.

And while we slept
deer came close.
We heard their breath.
We dreamed we were lost
and would stay there for good
together.

In the morning, before
you were up, I caught
a fish, held it
underwater
to feel my own body.
You woke. We spoke
hardly at all.

The length of a life.

I Live Alone

by counting blue
objects, then yellow,
then red. I'm burning,

I've said, inside. My wife,
who's color-
blind, tightens
my arm bones, ties them
back, while our children
bark for more.

Then she stamps, my wife.
Her blue eyes gnaw
what ache called love once,
cutting our tongues.

And I would still beg her
to pet me. I would
lick her, bleed,
and feel true love

isn't aching but arm bones
and blue eyes, but colors,
dear children, colors
need counting.

True Story

As he walked, each house he passed grew smaller. At first this surprised him; later it seemed almost natural. When he'd walked so far the houses were small enough to carry, he leaned as though over the first crocus of spring, took firm hold of a beautiful gingerbread, pulled it from the ground and slipped it into his overcoat. By the time he got home, his wife was inside. He scrunched up one eye and looked in through the downstairs living room window. Although he couldn't see her, he could see her clothes strewn around the tiny room. The book he'd been reading that morning lay on the floor by the comfortable-looking sofa; he could faintly smell his smells and hers. He shook the house gently, still looking in through the window. Nothing moved, not books, not clothes, not utensils on the table. Glued down. His wife, though, from the upstairs bedroom, cried out as she was thrown to the floor and against walls and ceiling. Her door was glued closed too.

Her voice, from such a tiny body, behind a glued door, was too small to hear.

Mercy, Mercy

Every time we argue
my wife becomes a horse.
Not a symbol or a dream.
A horse. There's nothing
I can do then but let her
run.

On her back I can hardly
breathe. I am ducking
branches and wires
as she races down the street.
Of course I can't talk now.
I hold tight to her mane

and beg mercy.
I am a simple man,
grateful to find myself
face down in the dust,
snakelike and coiled
as she rears and begs mercy.

And I sell it to her cheap.
One bite. Then we're a family.

Near Inverness, Florida

While you sat naked
sunning in a grass
path beside
the river, reading,

I perched on a leg-shaped
dinosaur cypress
log that kicked into
the black deep water—

Watched islands of water-
lilies float
past and thought
of the old, true

saying: "even
sitting on
a rock, five
years," and I sat still.

There were flowering lily
pads clustered
in the log's crotch;
their stems were filled,

when I peeled the green leather
away, with perfect
styrofoam hearts
I picked to show you.

And then I took off
my clothes. When we swam
our bodies disappeared
under the river.

No one knew us then.
If we had
vanished forever
we would have never been missed.

The cool root-
colored water
polished our bodies
as heavy fish

and snakes I imagined
pulled back into
a forest of roots
to watch, and the current

coaxed us gently,
imperceptibly toward
the turquoise sea
a hundred miles away.

My One True Story

The lake was covered with drowning bees
as I swam out, splashing a path, hoping
not to be stung, needing to be
refreshed, wondering how so many
bees had landed at one time in
the water, why they couldn't fly
free, whether this was a sign
that something had changed. And nothing flew.

My friends, naked, waved from shore
too frightened of bees to dive in, while I
watched the bees around me buzz
in circles through the water, stop
a moment, then buzz again. I waved
back, dove down and looked back up
at sky and the circling bees, swam
as far underwater as possible toward
shore, burst up for breath, then down
to swim in further, always looking
up at the bees, touching bottom to push
up for breath and a head covered

with bees. There were no hungry birds
in the air, no fat fish below;
I was alone, swimming down, bursting up,
forgetting even the bees and my friends, now
dressed, calling me to swim in
through the bees, a rug of yellow
across the lake. And then I remembered
flowers, honey, dove down to the rock
bottom to gather them: drowning: looking up.

Cocoon

In a town at the base of a hill, hidden
under tall grass, nestled in the roots
of a blossoming fruit tree, two boys play catch.
Each time they throw they grow older, taller,
more like their fathers, and each time they catch
they grow young again. The sound of the ball
in their mitts, no steady rhythm,
wakes sisters from windows, from flowers, and soon
the girls are running bases between their brothers,
who throw the ball higher as their sisters
run faster in their white dresses, blurring
into one girl, who turns as she runs
out of her breath, into butterflies and tiny birds
that fly in circles around the boys' heads
and away across the endless fields.

Hands

Today thousands
of envelopes filled
with tiny hands
are passing through the mail.

It is a sunny
day and all
these small hands sweat
in their mailman's bags.

These are the hands
of the skunks, squirrels,
raccoons that have now
become so valued

for their strangeness, for their
resemblance to ours.

Deep in the woods
there are still small animals
with all four hands.
They hide well. And all

around the edges,
close to our houses,
many walk on stumps.
They don't walk far.

We feed them scraps
from our dinners, and they
grow fat and sleek.
They sleep without fear.

Their hands will last
forever now.

Needing Silence

she walked out, leaving
her appliances purring—
stepped off her back steps
into a sudden

forest. Her husband
and children noticed
nothing.
And as she walked

she bit her wrists
to bleed a trail
back home.
She walked so far

she bit her hands off.
She left them in her path,
without regrets—
But just as suddenly

they grew back: flowers
in the moonlight, shocking her.
So she followed the perfume
in her new hands, was soon

forever lost.
She went about her family's lives
in the same old way:
cooked dinner, tucked them in,
read them fairy tales

while butterflies and dragonflies,
larger than she'd ever seen
before, surrounded her,
talking their strange

patter, flattering her.
She held up her hands,
a bouquet, as she walked,
and they drank her scent,

these insects, and got drunk,
or so it seemed,
the way they seemed to burn the air.
They danced like blossoms

falling from a fruit tree
in early summer wind
but they never fell.
Their fruit could never grow

if the blossoms never fell,
she thought. And for the moment
that was reassurance,
enough.

He Said

atoms remain unchanged, no matter
how many lives they are formed into
or how they are gathered into such forms.

All atoms on earth were here when earth
had borne only simple plants, rocks,
and pure blue sky. Long before. I love you.

And they will be here, unchanged, when there are
no more such forms, or anything we can
imagine. They will have taken other
forms, not necessarily real ones, he said,
by our standards. Purely abstract, maybe.

That was on our first date, and I was impressed.
I believed him. For some reason, my youth or my weak mind,
I followed him everywhere, my amateur physicist.

I was always trying to understand
how god fit into this concept, my god:
truth linked to truth in a great chain
to make the whole, this real world, make sense.

I never mentioned that part of me.

Before long we had children, lived their lives.
I developed no theory of my own.
He taught me everything—almost everything—I know.

So with our children gone and him
retired in front of the TV, I've started
talking—not talking
exactly—*communicating*
you could call it, with my atoms. I can't
explain how, but I do it. They listen,
that's all I know for sure.

I sit here while he dozes in his recliner, TV
blaring, and I talk softly to my atoms
about the lives they made me and the other lives they've made,
and I know in my deepest heart they hear me.
I know they will never forget me. They are me,
my deep me. He was right,

but he forgets himself already.
He's already scattered.

Who will live our billion lives?

Door

I open and close my favorite door
to hear the whine of hinges; it doesn't
lead anywhere, I think, but dark—
and anyway, I never go out:
I have binoculars, good eyes.

Though he never smiles he is always friendly
in his way. I catch the scent
of forest, pine needles, mushrooms when I open him,
sometimes when I stand close
and knock.
I think he's a bear sometimes when I wake late—

I wish he were. He could protect me.
And I could walk with him in the daylight, ask him questions
about how it feels. He never growls.
And in the morning he's just my door, good door—
through which, someday,
I'll leave.

Lion

–for Burton Raffel

Behind that door
in a white room we keep
a man who thinks
he is a lion.
You can see he's kept safe.
He thinks he's a lion!

Once he escaped
and ran through the city.
Disappeared.
Changed his name.
Actually this isn't him—
this is a lion.

And this is a picture
of the African plains.
We'll slip it beneath
his door now; he'll look at it
smiling, draw
an animal on it
and himself running
to catch it, slip
the picture back under
the door.

Thus we study
the workings of his mind.

Today he's drawn
a bowl, that's a bowl
of soup, being carried
by a stick figure, a woman.

That's him smiling.
Notice the hair
is wild, that he wears
no shirt.
Each day the picture
is different, but he always
smiles. Tonight his dinner

is soup, of course,
and a woman, but what
do you think of his smile,
his naked chest, skinny
after months in the white room,
but still wild—

What do you think
he dreams of, who do you
think he is, who do you think
he thinks
he is, we are? These are some
of the questions we ask ourselves.
A wild man! A lion!

I Met a Man in Here Once

He was dying, I think he said, from the birds
that kept struggling out of his bunched-up clothes.

They flew up and down the long room, barely
grazing the heads of us at the bar.

His face rolled around on top of his dark
jacket in the dark bar, and he talked very softly

as he struggled with his body. *Listen,* he said,
throwing a pigeon from his sleeve, slumping

lower, *everything is an animal. That's my understanding.*
Silence is an animal. I remember the wolves

I lived with before I left that situation
and the hawks these birds fly from. Look closely.

There are wolves behind everything. Bartender, please—
And so we got drunk. The birds were frantic.

They'd found perches on the rafters
and the lights and they argued

loudly while we drank. Snow fell outside.
The room had the glow streetlight reflected

on fresh snow makes coming in through iced windows.
By last round the birds were building nests, I thought,

and was grateful. But the next night they were gone.
I came early, pockets full of suet to charm them.

They were already gone. I come here every night.
I stand here drinking, and I listen to the animals

move around in my body, elegant and beautiful,
"mindless," and already near extinction.

I observe their passing.

3

from
Immaculate Bright Rooms (1994),
Many Simple Things (1997), and
Singing With My Father (2001)

Anniversary

The horse in our bedroom
came in with the flowers
we picked this early
morning together.

We noticed it first
when you started to sing.

What's left of our first born,
who rode as the sea
rides over the sea,
to another shore?

This horse is too big
for our cramped bedroom.

We will ride out tomorrow,
braid its mane
with flowers, turn it
back to the flowers.

Until then we will mount it
quietly, both of us,
here in this small room,
together.

Some Nights

when the moon is a knuckle in the dark, I kiss
my children sweet dreams, flick on their Little
Mermaid nightlight, deadbolt their doors,

and walk out beyond the dens
    of stiletto-heeled somnambulists,
out beyond the camps
    of the leather-bellied hip-hop dancers,
out beyond fish-breath, styrofoam, funky
seaweed, families of migrating hollow-boned,

past-life misogynists, sock-smellers, phosphorous,
a universe of duct tape, dealers in cat-gut,

spider-web wound-staunchers, reed blowers, musicians
of the human bone, families of the human bone,

stories which feel themselves vanishing, uncles
who have already vanished into memorized pop songs,
blossoming raven-haired heifer women, gasoline—

I walk beyond plastic Christmas trees flecked
with tinsel, filled with car exhaust, out beyond
ambulance, out beyond the muddy gut-thumpers,
out beyond: out beyond the oozing pelt of muck

into a place
    of tall grass and breeze
            and fireflies, where I
stand until morning,

watching constellations,
feeling my blood move,
hearing my blood move,
moving my blood.

This Poem

Once, waking early on a day of vacation,
full of plans and good intentions, and coffee, I saw

a car-wounded opossum in front of our house.
It just stood there in the middle of the street wagging

its over-heavy head, while cars transporting
their owners to work
honked and circled

slowly around. I stood inside
wanting him to die, to disappear, so I

could get to my reading, my plans, undisturbed.
I felt I should take control, go out there
and end his misery. He just kept standing there,

shuffling a little, shaking his oversized,
cracked-open head. I stayed inside all day

looking out at him. Of course he died
by evening, on my neighbor's side

of the street. I went out
to look at him then,

to apologize, to make myself feel less
guilty, less wimpy, to nudge him closer

to my neighbor's house, to maybe make a poem
out of all those things. But I thought I saw breathing,

so I went back inside, locked the doors, cranked the music
loud, the kind of music I hardly

listen to these days, music so cruel
it can make things disappear, and I did a kind of dance,

a kind of rocking back and forth
trance dance in my vacation house.

It worked.

Crows

1.
Last night a black bird
flew down my chimney,
fluttered on the floor
between us, broken,

then flew up into
your open mouth
which spoke on as if nothing
had happened.

"Are you all right?"
I asked, and as
I spoke, a flutter
of wings in my throat

as my black heart flew back up
the chimney, into
the night
and the still-falling snow.

2.
There are moments when feathers
that aren't good
for flying or good looks
cover my body

and I must stay
inside, plucking
the feathers, licking
the small drops of blood.

First Love

He catches a bird, holds it cupped
in his hands and calls her.
She leans.
He pulls his hands apart.

The bird flies into
her face, flaps
against her eyes,
and, stunned, falls.

He crushes it, smiling,
his back to her.
She hears the small bones break.
She leans over the bird

and sees it is still
breathing, fluttering
its broken bones.
And while he walks away

she carries a heavy
stone to cover it,
still blinking in the tall grass.
And then she runs after him.

Blue Feathers

This child broke his arm
falling from a tree—

And when the cast
came off, his arm
was covered with soft blue
feathers of a species
no one could name.

At first he seemed proud
as though growing one useless
wing were some sort
of accomplishment, as though
feathers were a mark
of individuality.

But lately he's silent
in oversized, long-sleeved
shirts; he sulks
though his arm works as well
as it ever has—

And the feathers are downy,
beautiful, hardly
visible, almost
ordinary hair.

From Day to Day

1.

The world is changing so fast
we hardly recognize ourselves
from day to day.

Some people
go to sleep as one self,
dream another, and wake
in a world that is familiar
but rearranged.
And by the time they catch up
with that world or themselves
it has all been rearranged again.

2.

To seem sensitive I claimed
to love the veins in leaves
when they looked like veins
in a human hand. She held my hand.

To seem compassionate I claimed
to love extinct birds
caught deep in the rings
of giant trees now being cut
for nothing important. We sang.

3.

I lost her one morning
when I forgot her name.

When I waved good-bye
I was not a tree
though I was covered
with leaves scribbled
with veins, admonished
by wind, with leaving.

Once I lost years
of my best past driving
home from work.

No snapshots remain.

Old Story

On an avenue of trees,
an orderly landscape
in bright birds, deep shade,
and breeze, I found myself

wanting to tell someone
special something
secret, to enter
that kind of wilder

landscape, so I kept myself
walking until
I entered a clearing
where night had already

fallen. Birds
were singing in their sleep.
I slept through many memories
and woke beside a woman

I'd slept beside for years
who led me back
along my path,
beneath constellations

she named until
they disappeared
and we were in someone's
light-filled home

I almost recognized.

A Dance Called Leaping

1.
Spring sunlight poured stillness
which refused to define her.

2.
Sunlight poured stillness
but here there were only
trees and whatever
could be derived from trees.

3.
Wind could be derived.

Her favorite stories were derived.

Even bread could be derived,
or so she'd heard. From sawdust.

Sap.

4.
Life could be derived
if she never stopped thinking
her body a huge
fiasco, or so

she'd been taught.
So she never stopped thinking.
She bruised herself to feel herself.

5.
Some windows were her body.

A Form of Emotion

He digs a pond
in his small garden,
plants rare species
there, and cultivates
fish, which he eats
sometimes, in a ritual
he's imagined makes some
connection between
that living water
and him.

There is such emptiness
at the heart of his story
that sometimes the grass
on his lawn won't lie down
when he walks across it.

He feels the tips
of the grass blades poke into
his bare feet, while bugs,
worms, and even snakes
look up at him
from the shade huts where they polish
their small, perfect eggs
and sing songs to their unborn
who will emerge suddenly,
looking exactly
like they do, knowing
everything they'll ever know.

"Abide With Me"

That first year together, we lived in the shadow
of a fishing line factory, next to a super
highway, under a railroad bridge,

beside a field of junked cars, mountains
of tires and hub caps and smashed glass, and we

prayed fervently, young lovers, for our love
to return this world to the poised grace we could still
imagine sometimes when we touched each other right,
imagine sometimes when we saw sunlight glint

on the stream full of minnows and beer cans and junk
that ran by the factory walls.

We prayed with our bodies. That year we could float things
in mid-air on the hymns we sang in perfect harmony.

We practiced one hymn—"Abide With Me"—
until we could lift cankered minnows from that stream,
until we could lift stray cats and junkyard dogs,
until we could lift each other as high
as our voices would carry. And then we sang stories—
we called them hymns—about our families,

our memories and secrets, until we could float
in unison, knowing that if either of us stopped singing
we would both fall. We were invisible,
or so it seemed. We were often happy.

We drove east that spring in a broken-down step van,
arguing and telling tales, sleeping in whatever dreams
we could sing each other. We walked beyond our own scent
somehow, one morning—it was in the north of Maine—

and watched a pair of loons or human beings learn to dance
on water, far out. The lake was dark and far too cold.

To summarize: We danced ourselves
through other shapes, and others.
To summarize: Eventually
we ate sweet butterflies and bees

and tamed ourselves by lying more
and more proficiently, creating
lives to come—and then we drove back
home, slowly, seeing all
the sights; and then we drove back home

again, singing and arguing, listening
for echoes of ourselves, with our eyes pinched tight.

There Was a Mother

gave birth to a bone
which grew a kind of flesh
and lived. There was a memory
grew hands and pulled itself
back into this world.

One kind of wind
blows just to blur things:
One kind of wind
scrubs us, makes us light
and shadow.

Another kind of wind
can't move.

One Language to Forget With

I came home one day and found our bed had vanished.
In its place was a plot of wildflowers all blooming
and my husband in the center of them, working at the ground
as though he were engaged in some hobby, like building
model trains or folksy little wooden toys
for our grandkids. He was kneeling there wearing a straw hat,
singing under his breath, squinting as though
the sun were bright, though he was in the house,
of course, in our bedroom. We're not so young
anymore and you can be sure I'm not going
to sleep on some couch in my living room, so I
clapped my hands. I called out. And he turned, smiling
with that inflated, self-involved sense of his own
goodness, and told me young guys from some group
of shell-shocked veterans had needed a mattress—
so he'd given it all, mattress, bed frame, bed—
for good karma, he said. Good karma! Since when
was he thinking about karma? And where will we sleep?
And how will those flowers survive in this
air-conditioned bedroom? We'll water them, he said,
and we'll hope. I plan to introduce a handfull
of bees tomorrow for their honey, honey,
and for the sound of their buzzing, which helps me dream.
And we'll sleep here, beside this rich field in this room
we've slept in for over thirty years, my love.
I still love you; I always have. You're more beautiful
now than you've ever been before, especially
in this small field of wildflowers. Here, attach

this hose to the bathroom faucet and we'll
create a fountain, or even a stream,
we can sit beside and marvel at while we tell each other
stories we both know so well we'll hardly have to listen.

Modern Dance

He listened to his wife moving around the house
humming as she banged things, as she opened doors,
stepped in and closed them behind her, to emerge
from other rooms, muttering in various languages.
He imagined, as he lay there dozing, that his wife
was painting their windows black, so she could
tell him some difficult secret, so she could
take off her clothes beneath her clothes,
ask for something that way, silently.

A Simple Tree

One of the last times I saw her, my grandmother
took me out to lunch, ordered us both
daiquiris, sipped hers with gusto, and started
laughing loudly. She leaned then and whispered
a story she claimed to have just remembered
about my father as a boy, trying on her lipstick
to see if it would make him talk differently, know
larger words—and she laughed even harder
at that memory, until she was almost crying.
The restaurant had a big picture window which looked out
at a well-tended lawn and some large oak trees.
My grandmother nodded, still laughing, still crying,
and told me *that world out there isn't*
the world anymore, though it was what it was
when your father was a boy. I don't know what you'll do
when the angels in those trees decide not to let you
climb up there and sing and the whole way of life
we've planted here withers away. I'm glad
I won't see it come. I want to be a tree,
I've wanted that a long time. Just to be a simple tree.
She smiled then and closed her eyes and sighed
softly, and then she fell asleep
before she'd even ordered. So I ate alone.

Certain Trees

The old Cuban tree man
who walked around our neighborhood,
clipboard in hand, inspecting our trees,
told me, in Spanish, to cut back our aging
key lime, to keep it
alive a few more years.
Even strict pruning, he said, might not do any
good, for the tree had lost its *sense
of jubilation*. He squinted at the bare branches
and told me to paint whatever wounds
I cut, to seal the rot out, to protect
the old tree's heart; then he thanked me graciously
and moved next door, to examine our neighbor's
stunted avocado, and on down the street.

That afternoon, while I climbed up into
the old tree with saw and paint can, my wife
planted a forest, no bigger than our double bed,
of slash pine and tall-grass susans, blue daze,
hardy-looking, button-perfect, purple creeper flowers
whose name I don't know; then she watered the dwarf
cypress the mocking birds love so to perch in,
to survey the neighborhood, calling witty insults
at humans and cats, copying everybody's
songs, until their constant mocking

becomes like our bodies if we don't touch each other
enough, just part of the landscape we inhabit,
which is hardly even noticed anymore, sometimes
for years, like the roar of jets
or traffic, or the groaning of freight trains in the small
hours, when you might as well be sleeping.

Moon Flowers

This is the hour when opossum shuffle
up to our back door to poke around

in our garbage and teach their pouched kittens how
to play dead; this is the hour when worms

pull themselves from our apples, to slide
across our counter tops, when foxes

comb each other's tails beneath
the yellow lights in our alley, and snails

take the slow journey
across our front porch;

this is the hour when flowers shaped
like baby's fists or ears open

their faces and sing, in voices only
the lightest of human sleepers can hear.

Yearning to Be Beautiful

> *As bees buzzed and wood pigeons cooed, you*
> *could listen to God's creation and take pleasure*
> *in its subtle variety.*
> —Robert Lacy: *The Year 1000*

It rains every day in this season, and in every
raindrop, I could believe, are tiny fish or frogs

that swim or hop or wriggle away
into the ground or the trees. Things

are coming alive all around me, yet I am
afraid in some place before language, as when

I became a self, aware of my separate
being, and thought *this is me*, much later

in life than my ancestors must have, who couldn't
linger so long in childhood and must have

lived a different-sounded self,
in a silent time, where spirits

might have been heard in the fluttering leaf
and a year lasted longer than it does now. But I grew up

slowly, at the edge of a huge city, free
to roam our neighborhood of grass and swamps

and remnant woods, places where we could
pretend to be wild, stalking whatever

we imagined, hunting invisible things.
We've vanished, of course, into what we are today.

And today it is raining; green things are growing quickly;
flowers are bursting into fragrances we should be

drugged by: Things that can't think might be
beautiful forever; conscious things

can be beautiful only in brief moments of
awareness, balance, stop-time: into

wind and pollen, green stuff, spider webs
and rain filled with millions of mindless, dreamless

tiny-souled creatures that vanish into everything
even as the rain falls, as we all are vanishing,

conscious of our vanishing, watching ourselves
go, yearning to be beautiful.

Midsummers: The Sound

–for my father

Many summers, around mid-July,
when the days were stifling, hazy and still,
the cul-de-sac of harbor we lived beside
filled with thousands of slack-gray, foot-long
fish, mossbunkers, chased in by the bigger
open-water blues. The mossbunkers pressed into
the harbor, thrashing against each other
for space, until their thrashing depleted
the water of oxygen; then they gasped
to the surface, twisted in circles, slapped
the water with their tails, turned belly-up
and died. The bluefish slashed at them then
until their entrails curled out into the water—.

My father would come home from work and take
a swim in that harbor water, even
when it was crowded with suffocating fish:
He'd ignore them or breaststroke-splash them away,
swim out to a moored sail boat, hold on there
a moment to catch his breath, and swim back,
immensely pleased with himself. Then,
dripping, he'd examine his roses in the evening
that was filled with the sounds and stench of thrashing
fish. He'd pick a few ripe tomatoes,
sip his whiskey, check the coals
in the grill, and go inside to get
whatever he was cooking, or to put some jazz
on the record player: bebop: Monk or Bud Powell.

I remember fireflies, those nights we sat outside
to eat. I remember the breezes that sometimes cleared
the fishy air so we could smell
whatever was blooming, breathe the green life
of summer. I remember the dull clang of ropes
against aluminum masts, the hourly
chime of church bells, the muffled metallic
roar of the commuter trains a mile
or so away, across the harbor
and town. I tried to imagine those trains,
full of strangers and light, as I lay in my bed
those nights of my childhood when I knew as little

as I do now about anything that matters, when I felt
most deeply my lack of understanding
and so had to make up my life. Sometimes

I woke late and listened to my parents thrashing
about the house, mumbling, and I wanted
to understand something, so I got up,
stood at the head of the stairs, and listened—
phosphorescent in the dark—and I saw them in their night selves,
moon-fleshed and primitive. Then I turned back
to bed and tried to think up a story
that could make things make sense, until I fell
asleep again. And I think I slept for years,
as the old stories tell us we do, and I dreamed
lives I must have forgotten by the time
I woke again, tangled up inside
my own body, which was so potent
and well oiled, those days, it seemed capable of taking
any shape it called itself, of becoming anything—.

Loons

One rainy late summer afternoon in Maine
my father and I took a sauna together
in the woods, by ourselves;
then we swam in the cold lake,
too far out for me; my father just kept on
swimming. I followed. There was mist across the lake,
and I worried that he might disappear, that I might forget
the direction to shore. And then, just as
I called out I couldn't keep up, that I was turning back,
we swam up against a huge rock, almost
an island, submerged just beneath the surface.
We pulled ourselves out and surveyed the mist
over the water: We couldn't see the shore
or hear anything but our own bodies. The rain
had stopped. We stood there breathing, naked,
when my father started talking, hesitantly
at first, about loons, about their mournful songs,
about how rare they are, how rarely they allow
any human to see them. They mate for life,
he said. Then he told me other things I wish
I could remember, and then he kissed me
between my shoulder blades, sat down on the edge
of that rock so only his shoulders and head
were above the water—while I stood, a skinny boy,
beside him—and then he pushed off, from that sitting
position, slipped into the water, and swam
back with his sure stroke, stopping only once
to gesture to me, to follow.
That night I slept on the screened porch, inside
the exuberant, billion-throated calls of just-born

frogs, inside the scribble of fireflies,

the echo of owl hoot, silence, and the mournful

calls—way out in the mist—of loons,

which kept me awake, though I tried not to listen.

Light

For over a year when I was a young man,
night never fell. We lived inside closets
for the darkness, or underneath
beds, and we grew
deliriously tired. Eventually we dreamed
while we went about our lives, while we talked to each other,
and lived a kind of double life, dreaming and waking
at the same time, even when we drove our cars,
even when we talked or touched each other.
Gradually, we almost forgot about darkness,
in less than a year. Night creatures starved.
Crops grew heavy in half the normal season,
children went to school double time, and we worked
just to do something, and we grew thin just living,
and we grew old more quickly,
bleached pale from all that light.

4

from
*Sleeping With the
Lights On* (2000)

Mushrooms

Your wife lies on her back, breathing deeply in sleep, naked beneath a heavy quilt. She smells like warm hay. The bedroom is silent but for the ticking of your wind-up alarm clock and the window panes, which rattle in the wind. You have been reading by the light of a candle you lit before making love, hours ago it seems now. The candle is little more than a pool of wax, a sputtering light throwing shadows on the wall. You put your book on the floor, turn toward your wife, and pull down the quilt. Then you rake your fingernail across her belly, just below the rib cage, to draw a faint red line. Taking a deep breath, and squinting, you peel back the skin below the breastbone, reach up to your elbow into her body, behind the lungs and heart, into the mossy sponge back there, and pull out mushrooms that glow in the dark. You know that if you eat them you will not be able to sleep for days, that you will turn hairy inside your body, so you hold them up and simply run your tongue across their slimy skin, finally sucking the juice, the glowing light, out of them. Then you place them beneath your pillow and collapse into your sleep. As soon as you start to breathe deeply, she wakes, takes your hands and arms and begins stuffing you into her body, through the hole you cut. She pushes you all the way in before you wake; then she takes the sputtering candle and drips hot wax across her belly, sealing you inside, where you've always wanted to be. Blowing out the candle then, she turns back to her sleep.

Song for the Other Half of My Body

...to sleep with my invisible ...
        –Michael Burkard

I want to sleep with my invisible, she told me, smiling. I want to sleep inside a photograph that holds us in a deep blue bed. We could drown there, maybe, in a photograph taken from the angle of profile I could cut my face into, the way you cut yourself shaving sometimes, a place where there is always a glistening breeze. And we'd imagine that breeze had traveled centuries across salt water that is teeming, even today, with migrating mammals who travel with the devouring speed of absolute innocence, innocence that passes before we can see.

I want to trade arms with my invisible, she said more loudly, to trade leg bones and dance: such sweet dreams between us, a small blue flame we eat to grow warmer than we've burned for years. Then I'll eat colored glass smoothed by the weight of deep water, by the rhythm of waves. I want to eat perfect shells and smile up at my invisible swimming above me, a boat or cloud-shadow against the naked sky.

I want to grow bright scales, she said, to grow fur and sing in that howl language with my very own invisible. I want to take the long journey across those bleached sheets we wrap around ourselves when we yearn to grow into one person, that which is not and the gradually vanishing, a snapshot of light our best portrait. So we stretch ourselves to air. We stretch ourselves to silence. We pretend to stretch into each other. We might pretend our lives.

When the breeze shifts direction even slightly, she whispered, the small animals we believe in but have never really seen, the small animals we've given no names to yet, the perfect creatures that might not actually exist, these little *beings* wake suddenly in the real tree outside our window. They look around for a moment, I think, and then they fall back to sleep, still unnamed, still invisible. Their breath is regular and constant, day and night. Their breath is soothing; I breathe with them to fall asleep.

And their dreams are only color and light: blue sometimes, but mostly simple white.

Breathing Underwater

She claimed it was impossible for her to laugh in the morning. She said in the morning she felt lonely for the wonderful relationships she carried on in dreams, friendships she'd maintained for years, *through all my changes*. She said it was hard, just *hard*, to even smile after leaving them in there and moving through this waking world, this unforgiving place where objects feel solid but break so easily, forever. *By noon I'm all right*, she said then; *by noon I've reassured myself that I'll find everyone well when I fall back to sleep tonight*. She flushed a little, smiling. I didn't want to tell her I rarely remember any dreams, that even when I do remember some moment from my sleeping, it disappears as quickly as I remember it. So I changed the subject. We'd met by chance a week or so earlier and fallen into a long discussion of whatever came to mind; I don't remember now exactly what we talked about, but I do know we walked a long distance, that we stopped at some point for coffee and then stopped a little later for wine, that we'd left each other reluctantly, at dawn. I hadn't told her I was color blind, and I hadn't yet told her the whole world smelled fresh and permanent when I was with her. I couldn't find the words, but it was true: Everything smelled as clean and eternal as a cool jasmine-blossom night when she was beside me, when we walked and when I listened to her talking; and the things we passed while we walked, houses and trees and even cars, had sensuous presences, wonderful to breathe. Then she claimed I'd shown up in her dreams, that I'd taken off my clothes there and displayed my sleek body. She claimed my dream body was furred and purred, *though you're definitely human;* she claimed my dream body had wings when I needed them: Then she told me she could swim underwater *as far as I can sleep, which goes down as deep as the solid darkness at the core of things.*

Waking to Rain

*I thought about the secrets our bodies have, what they
keep from us. Our bodies have lives of their own.*

–John Dufresne

When I was a child, my hands would sometimes fall off and get lost
in the grass or in my house somewhere—and I would have to search
for them, sometimes late at night, when everyone else was sleeping.
I'd be lying in bed, starting to drift off, when I'd need to touch my own
body, and I'd realize my hands were missing. So I'd lie there trying
to remember back to when I'd used them last. After awhile I'd get up,
get dressed as best I could without hands, and I'd walk around the
dark house, out into the yard and street, looking for my hands, calling
out—until at last I found them. Once I lost my hands for a whole winter
afternoon when I hadn't worn gloves. They had to be thawed out slow-
ly, under lukewarm water. They ached for days. Another time I lost them
in a puddle in a thunderstorm, and by the time I found them they were
milk-colored, swollen, clumsy, and heavy—like waterlogged wood.
Once I lost a hand when I was body surfing; and once my right hand
snapped off in the grip of one of my father's business associates, a man
who believed in shaking with authority. No one noticed, of course,
except me. And I yearned to learn an instrument, to sing and play
music—but I couldn't train my hands, couldn't trust them to follow me.
Most sports were pure embarrassment. Of course I never flew a kite!
Picture me walking home from elementary school: I'd drop a hand like
a kleenex, without noticing until I'd reached home and I wasn't able
to open the front door. By that time my lost hand had usually crawled
away somewhere hard to find. So I kept my hands in my pockets and
I tried not to let go of anything. Later, when I started dating, I dreamed
I'd let my girlfriend keep my hands overnight as a token of my love,
and I imagined my hands lying on her bedside table, beside the glass

of water and the book of Rod McKuen poems I'd given her. Sometimes I imagined my girlfriend took my hands into the shower, into the bubble bath with her. She talked to my hands as though they were sweet dolls; she scrubbed my fingernails; she traced my life line. Then she used my hands to wash everywhere I imagined while I hurt myself with blunt wrists in the potent dark.

Boy with Two Tongues

...that old story of the boy with two tongues, who lived for years beneath his parents' house without anyone knowing: At night while his parents slept, he woke and pulled himself through some passageway, up into their house, where he walked around happily, watched TV, ate whatever he could find. Sometimes he dug through his parents' laundry hamper, trying on the soiled clothes he found there; sometimes he crawled beneath his parents' bed and whispered. He loved to listen to his parents breathing. As he grew older he sometimes slipped into bed between his parents. They smelled like fur. If either of them woke up briefly in the middle of the night, he held his breath and didn't move. When he wasn't moving he felt as though he could easily disappear, really disappear. But hadn't he already been gone for years? Where was he? Outside were night creatures and the small birds that flew only in moonlight, with faces he recognized when he stood in that outside darkness, which was so different from the darkness he usually inhabited. All those animals were running and flying around, talking whatever languages they spoke in those days, and the boy could understand them, and he could talk back to them with his double tongue. That night-talking felt like magic; that night-talking felt like purest happiness. And soon the animals learned to recognize his voice, learned to understand his language; they came out of their own species darkness, and they gathered around him. And slowly but surely, he became their listening....

Moving Bodies

There's no one else home, so you walk around your large house from room to room and around again, touching familiar objects, touching yourself, humming, thinking thoughts that disappear as soon as you think them. Your body feels well-muscled and sleek under your new clothes, and you think about that, too, as you walk around, think about how strange and distant your body sometimes seems to you, how deeply its functions fascinate even as they distance you from it, your body, the only ground you're sure your self knows, if indeed it knows anything at all. And right now in a distant city, in an office at the top of a glinting skyscraper, a woman you wouldn't even recognize remembers how you danced one mid-winter afternoon, by yourself in the middle of a waxed gymnasium floor, to the Spanish music from the janitor's transistor radio, how you twirled and smiled and then looked across the gym at her, suddenly embarrassed, turned and walked away. And she looks out her window, down across the city, and she sees you clearly, the way you turned away, and she feels again the urge to run after you, to grab your arm, to ask you please to dance with her. And even as she thinks of you, whose name she's probably never known, you hear a *salsa* melody, you start dancing in your living room.

Sounds Instead of Dreaming

I remember the whispering, like breeze, of sap freezing inside the huge tree in our back yard. And I remember the prickly feeling of someone's breath on my neck when I went alone into the wire woods out back, when I went out and down into the frozen swamps where all those other children lived—children with snow for eyes and breath of burning plastic. And so I loved old stories. I loved the smell of dirt and gasoline. I loved breeze across the cattails, across marsh grass when the tide was high. Then one cold New Year's Eve a little girl showed me a long chunk of styrofoam hidden in the marshes; and even though the winter was metallic and hurt, we took off our shoes and stepped on that tippy raft, pushed off into the harbor, out across the freezing. And soon we were falling, with the falling tide, out to what we never dared call *sea*, never called *ocean*, never called anything but *maybe* and *beyond*, where the appetite we'd never met could find its satisfaction, where the dark doors we dreamed of were always wide open. Afraid of tipping over, we couldn't move at all; we froze in one position and waited for the tide to turn. Since we didn't dare talk, we told each other silent stories. And since we told each other silence, we fell in love. When we got home, finally, it was almost next year. But no one seemed worried. No one seemed to have missed us. So my true love with the yellow tongue and burning flavor kissed me. Then she held my hand. Her hand was warm, though she hadn't worn gloves all those hours on the water. At the touch of her sure, warm hands, I fell ever more deeply, more inarticulately, in love. My own hands were numb with cold, curled on themselves and sharp as claws.

During the Cold War

I'm no longer sure
that what's important
is more important
than what's not...
    –Wislawa Szymborska

It was always late afternoon. As usual, we were waiting for my father. There was a tiger, my mother said, in her closet, way back behind everything. *Come with me . . . behind my clothes with me . . .* She held out her hand and we went back there together, down a winding damp trail through woods, stood watching this huge flame pace back and forth behind some window. *Window?* No, it was a cage; I'm sure now: I remember daring my hand through the bars. . .a yellow warmth. *Pull your hand back!* The whole closet glowed. How old was I then? My mother's face looked harsh, looked angry in that tiger light, but she turned to me, smiling. There was a smell of candle wax, of wet hair, of moth balls. . .She smoked a cigarette and cried softly and tried to smile at me. Then she threw her cigarette through the tiger's bars, held out her hand—which glowed now like the tiger's body—and led me back through the closet darkness toward home.

We came out hours later, but it was still the same late afternoon. When a jet passed, very low and loud, we got down on our knees and covered our heads, my mother and I, the way I'd been taught in the air raids at school. I showed her the proper way to kneel, how to tuck her chin against her breast and wait. She breathed loudly, and she told me she loved me. I told her I loved her too. *Just wait a little longer.* And then the jet was gone. The air filled with an awkward silence that wasn't quite relief. We stood up and smiled at each other. She hugged me. She sang me a lullaby and I closed my eyes…

When I woke, it was dark. I heard my father and mother talking, faint voices from the kitchen, talking gently of the day. I lay there awhile and listened, calm in my self, thoroughly content. I thought: *I am alone here, alone in my body...*

I could smell our dinner cooking, something Father loved to eat.

One Morning

you wake to find you can't move your tongue, can't decide what you're supposed to do when you wake up. And so you just lie there watching sunlight lengthen across the bedroom floor, listening to the radio chatter out the news, wondering who you've been, who you might be. After an hour, you get up, open a closet of women's clothes, shoes, and perfumed dresses. You step in there a moment and breathe deeply, trying to remember. You are naked. Do you live alone? Outside looks blurry, too bright, an unfocused photograph of someplace you almost remember. And when the phone rings, you pick it up and try to say *hello*. Someone far away says *mom,* says *mom,* says *mother, where have you been?* You put the receiver down without hanging it up and then you dress slowly, running your hands across your body, humming softly. Later, you step out into the blurry summer afternoon and walk briskly, eyes focused on the ground.

Tennis

Once I found a broken-winged mocking bird beneath our bed when I was awakened too early by someone I knew only slightly, calling to ask if I'd like to play tennis before the day grew too hot. I stood there naked saying *sure* before I thought about it, looking over with yearning at my sleep-swollen wife, hearing a small puffing thud from underneath our bed: This injured bird was mocking the flaccid sound of human sleep-breathing as it threw itself against our mattress, relentlessly attacking the seams and cotton batting. My wife slept on while I pushed a broom under there, trying to make the bird come out where I might catch it. And what would I do when I caught it, what then? Set it free? Toss it up into the air and watch it fall? So after awhile I just left it under there—I was afraid I would wake my wife with my racket; I knew the fierce bird would probably die soon anyway; and I reminded myself that my wife was better with wild birds than I was. She was better with her hands, just better at touching things. Her naked body on the bed there almost distracted me as I pulled on my whites, but then I heard my opponent at the door. We warmed up quickly and played with fierce enthusiasm. Then we rested and played some more. The day was so hot we lost track of the hour, we wore ourselves thin with running. By the time I got home my children were all grown up, my wife had packed and moved out, taken what was hers, remarried and moved away. She hadn't left a note. The TV was blaring the same talk show as usual, but everything else in the entire house was gone.

Everything, and Nothing At All

There's a train behind everything these days, like a humming tattoo underneath your skin, like the motion of emotion from love at first sight to the wood-like grain in the dream of loss. My brother is wading in a glass-littered stream over by the window we planted by the door. Do you hear him? He's singing, or cawing like some engine I've installed wrong in the back of my own head, a gimmick to watch myself watching things. We all stay the same, my good friend says, but our children keep getting bigger and older and strange. We're in that limbo period, changing inside where the whirring happens, where the gurgles never stop. And the fire you wore behind your eyes has faded now with the blue as the blue itself seeps out of things entirely, rendering us blunt and nearly confused. Memory exists outside the boundaries of your silence, eating the hallways darker, yielding nothing. How are you? Whoever are you? Mildew creeps across our teeth, where night swells new. I loved you when you spoke to me by simply muttering "you're silly, silly," and I loved you when you used my name as though it were a thing, utilitarian. Who are we, anyway, in this little life? I woke up in my bedroom and felt the dew soaking my hair. Who glances into you, sharp as any instrument, when the colors have just started fading into dusk? A tambourine is beaten by a crowbar in a virgin wood while someone you lust for collects eggs in the shadows. So you sing the mandolin song your mother improvised the moment you were born, the exact moment, in fact, you fell between her legs. Memories become you like trees become a forest, never making any noise unless the wind blows. Soon we will have vanished. We know there is nowhere to go but into the grain of things, into the dirt. Still, your teeth would feel good at the back of my neck, your fingers would feel sexy in my ribcage. So I offer you all the songs I know by heart, all the news I've created by simply living, a handful of glances and rebuffs. How many hours could you dance, she asked, without falling down or melting like snow? Whose life depends on it, I asked her then. Your own! Then I would dance for ninety years, then fall into that dark beyond that dark which is beyond. I'd say I love you. I'd tell you the self in my dreams is a grass man, a glass man, a song that found body by singing and then sang harmony and then harmony again—until, within these strands of song a body appeared, feathered and scaled and covered with human hair, afraid of everything and nothing at all.

Independence Day

The first half was sung by wind-through-the-trees, which was very like a woman on a rocky cliff above our lake. My real mother sailed in a dinghy down below, sailed in her good girl uniform that first summer, sailed naked and hairy by the time she went to college, by the time she met my father and made him summon me. And my mother made yearning sing like a yellow bird, so the days were endless and lost behind lost. Then who was this other body of another little boy, who could pull back the air or the ground we walked across or the glassy lake we swam in; who was this mere lad who could pull any skin back and enter things completely? Was he the music that makes the world stay? But then he'd grow silent, as good as never was. So I asked my dad: Why are we, anyway? And he said to make time happen; and then he said to love. Am I living in my body or is body what I am? I'm not sure, he told me, yet breathing makes the wind. Then one morning, much later, my wife turned to me and said: I woke beside a dog. I mean it was a wolf. I mean, I get lost in your skinny sometime wilderness. And then she touched me. Outside, I reminded her, the bees are making body parts from the pollen they've gathered. We might harvest it this afternoon, sweeten our love potion, and make our own honey in the bushes. Sure. But aren't we wild enough already, she wondered, aren't our bones more ourselves the more we memorize? Like sliding down a snowy mountain peak on Independence Day, when everyone else is in the city lighting fireworks and your brother is still living in a cave and your sister is making little plaster casts of her children's body parts, so she will remember them just as they never were.

Ordinary Bruises

For years, someone lived in my bedroom with me, someone with oily black hair that curled up at the nape of his neck and tattoos on his forearms, who chewed ice cubes and snapped chewing gum. He slept beneath my bed or behind my curtains or in my closet, and he never responded when I called out.

Then one night he was gone. The room smelled different. I stayed up late, as usual, reading another novel about my life to come. As I read, I pulled a single coarse black hair that curled just below my bellybutton. I pulled and it just kept coming, just kept growing longer. And the feeling was brand new, better than anything I'd felt before—

When I'd finished the novel a nest of black hair lay beside me on the mattress. I cut it with a cuticle scissors and hung the heavy coil of hair on a nail in my closet. I was hungry that morning, not at all tired, filled with a new story, a version of my life to come.

—And when I got married the first time, I gave my bride that coil of hair, from which she wove a negligee which revealed everything it covered. I never told her where that thread had come from, as she never told me where she learned to dance. She loved to paint my body with lipstick, to paint her nipples and bellybutton, to sing in a language I never learned, an "automatic" tongue, while she danced around me, poking me, taunting me with that blood-colored lipstick as she danced.

My second wife loved fishing nets, motorcycles, fishnet stockings. She thought she'd shaped our children from clay she dove for, down to the bottom of the lake we dreamed, behind the house we built with our bare hands. We grew old together, she and I, pinned back each other's faces and slack bodies, made each other new again that way.

Then we made love and unmade love until I was perfectly bald and covered with heart-shaped tattoos that are fading, even as we speak, into ordinary bruises.

Prolonging the Daylight

The absence of wind seemed to prolong the daylight we cherished
so, having lived so long closed up in our rooms, doing our small jobs.
And so we sat out there on that broad lawn, talking about anything that
came to mind, savoring that light, that stillness. Our very voices and
words seemed to keep the light in place. The time was getting late,
was turning toward night, but still we stood in calm, unchanging light
that seemed to rise from everything around us. We hardly knew each
other, and yet we felt comfortable when we gestured, when we talked
about feelings and memories. *Our bodies are preparing to vanish even
now*, an attractive woman mentioned casually, smiling at me. There
were tiny blue-and-yellow flowers in the grass, and when I turned to
look closely, to pick one and give it to this woman I'd just met, who
was talking so softly now about waves, about salt air, about solitude
and breath, when I leaned down to gather a thumbnail-sized wild
flower of a type I'd never noticed before, she started singing, started
chanting—and it sounded like her one voice contained harmonies, and
it felt like I was imagining her singing, that I'd imagined even her, the
mother of children we had never had together. I pulled the tiny flow-
ers, stood up, smiling, and gave them to her—but she looked suddenly
annoyed, leaned toward my drink and whispered: *We live midway
between everything, our own atoms and the stars.* As though that ex-
plained anything, as though that made me love her less. And then she
walked away, without looking back, to join some other group of strang-
ers, to whisper some other naive profundities. Perhaps she thought I'd
follow her for more. Perhaps I did.

The Longest Train in the World

The longest train in the world takes all night to pass. It is full of oddly-shaped boxes and cattle lowing at the moon. Commuters in their cars, heading home from work, are backed up to the horizon, miles beyond miles. The train moves slowly. You wonder who she is who sits in the car beside you, swaying back and forth to music from the radio. So you slide over into the passenger seat, open your window, and lean out: *Excuse me, would you like to come into my car and talk, I think we might be here awhile.* Smiling, she obliges. And soon the train appears to be a river and your car seems exquisitely comfortable; the full moon shines down on you, young lovers making music in the living dark, smelling each other up and down, making the air inside your old car thick with funk and deepest body oils. And when the longest train has passed, finally, you step out into the morning and walk hand in hand, half-dressed, hardly talking, abandoning your cars to the middle of the road, abandoning the narratives your lives have written up till now.

At My Brother's House

–For J.H.

My brother has difficulty reading my lips when we walk, so we stand still and watch a hummingbird hover in the air between us, drinking nectar from flowers we can't see, that cover invisible vines we might climb into the clouds, if our language were capable of bringing us to that pitch of understanding. There's a river, he tells me, that runs from the roots of the big trees on the hill behind his house. He tells me it rushes, like silence, beneath his house; sometimes it rises to run through his basement; once it rose high enough to carry him away. *For a few days.* He smiles. He's gone deaf, and he can't read my lips, he says, and he can't read my face. As a child he dreamed he could fly, and he hid once for days amidst the high trees that shaded our family. Another time he lost himself in the oily water of the busy harbor behind our house; he swam back home, calling out to me, but I was somewhere else, preoccupied with other thoughts and needs. Later that year the salt harbor froze solid; we went sliding in his little plastic dinghy in the silent freezing morning stillness. *It's never been that cold since then!* That year there were swans in the air each time the snow fell and the snow fell each time we looked at the sky, lost in our little lives, safe and laughing, hugging each other in the memorable cold.

Song

–for Bob Arnold

He dreamed the girl he loved turned into a tree outside his bedroom window, where, in winter, she flowered with snow and in spring and summer she flowered with blossoms that sometimes looked like butterflies and left a fragrance in his clothes. He dreamed he gathered her blossoms where they fell and made a pillow, and he dreamed he slept beneath that tree until his clothes tattered and fell away, until his skin tattered and fell away, until his own nerves or yearning reached into the ground and anchored him there. Then, he dreamed, he drank through his body and lived in slow time, almost forever, blossoming beside his love, mingling his scent with hers.

5

from
*The Point of
Touching* (2002), and
*Behind Our
Memories* (2003)

Christmas in the Woods

Our twelve-year-old daughter walks around the cabin
wearing a red velvet sweater with a fake zebra
collar and silky underpants, singing.
Her toenails are bright red. Outside, small birds
flit through the trees in the gray light, and beyond,
down the bluff, the river pulls.

The radio in the bedroom is tuned to a discussion
of refugee repatriation in various
unfamiliar countries. In the kitchen, my wife washes
dishes and sings Christmas carols with our daughter.
I pour us more coffee. Yesterday, a friend explained
the coming extinction. He shared all the details:

Squirrels and weeds, he said, and pigeons
will be our wildlife. Since then I've been making
lists of what I need to see. My son has started videotaping
everything we do and say, as though he might save us that way.

And so I'll sing with my wife and daughter—
smiling at the camera, in this cabin in the woods—
to celebrate the season, and to remind us,
someday, how happy we were.

Fruit Trees and Flowers

–for Matthew Hettich

That May night, almost midnight, when the doctor caught him,
my son looked at first like a seal-child, head pointed,
dark-furred and sleek, not yet fully human.

I panicked for a moment; then I took my first breath
as a father, and I saw him there, and I knew him. When he nursed,

the room filled with his light—
       and though I tried stubbornly
       not to let the nurses
       carry him away,
to prick and measure his perfect, perfectly
innocent body, they took him anyway.

I've planted fruit trees and flowers in my yard,
key lime and gardenia, hibiscus and muscadine.

They will offer flowers, fragrances and fruits
when their season comes, regardless
of how well I care for them
or anything I do.

Holding Tight

Lately, these first hot summer nights, pale-green frogs,
the size of a human hand, jump against our bedroom windows
and hang on for awhile there, pushing their panting
green bellies flat against the pane. We notice them,
most nights, while we are undressing, talking softly,
or reading drowsily in bed.
Sometimes I put my palm against the pane,
standing naked in the sleepy room, as my wife turns off
the reading light and slips between the sheets. I imagine
I might feel that belly; I might feel that cool breathing.

Then, lying together, just before sleep,
we listen to the frogs hop or fall off our windows,
one by one; we listen to them push themselves
off into the ferns, where they start their peculiar
croaking as we fall into sleep, curled
around each other, breathing each other's
breathing, beginning
already to dream.

Memorable Food

We went fishing one Sunday that winter my brother
was in a wheelchair. The day was clear glass.

He caught an eel—as long as our father's arm—
which refused to die. He had caught it, so we took it

home, to eat. And though our mother
smashed its head with brick and hammer,

it still flailed.
And when she chopped its head off

with the dull hatchet
my father used for kindling,

it flailed more wildly, spewing blood
all over the walls of our kitchen, the windows,

our parents. By the time it finally
lay still, it was bruised and flaccid, flattened

beyond recognition, the color of intestines.
—And then our parents broiled and ate it,

with garlic. *Delicious* they called out, coughing
into their napkins, chewing and coughing

and calling out enthusiastically to thank my little brother
for catching such *interesting,* such *memorable* food.

The Small Bird

When no one was watching, she chewed handfuls of the dry
leaves her father raked to burn.
Her mother was hanging the sheets out in the wind
that leapt from the ground and made her dress fly up.
The leaves flew up around her father's legs.
He told stories as he raked, about how he'd once been
a field of lean grass and wildflowers blowing
in an autumn wind, like this one; he'd been mist across a lake
at dawn when the cormorants swam underwater
without making a sound.
He said he'd met her mother when she was just an unsung song.
You see what I mean? Our lives are anything
but solid. But still they are real.
The distance between any two things, he reminded her,
is infinite. Everything is infinite. She started
laughing then, as she remembered him climbing
a ladder up into his favorite apple tree,
filling his shirt with tart apples, then climbing down,
smiling, offering her an apple but giving her
a small bird instead, which he'd clutched in his fist
and which she'd kept since then, and which she still held tight.

Watching My Children Sleep

Lost in woods
I imagined I came upon
a doe at a small creek
who turned to look calmly
at me and refused
to run.

There were tiny flowers growing
from her body, forget-me-nots
that glowed in the woods-dusk
as I reached out

to touch her. As I touched her
she fell away into stone—.
Her legs became roots
jutting out into the creek.

I lay down across her
and drank the icy
delicious water.
Then I gathered those flowers

from what had been her body
to light my way back home.

Insomnia

My wife believes certain
specifically balanced
aromas can cure us.
She believes in sound
therapy, touch
therapy, vibrational
medicine.
She believes in good thoughts.
She believes in conscious breathing.

Tonight, I listened
to the small breezes swirling
our back yard, thought
of a tree I might plant
for its flowers, and listened
to the usual midnight
freight train, groaning
like the things in ourselves
we can't keep ourselves
from returning to.

I wonder if anyone
walking by our house
through the dark dark of almost
dawn could see me
sitting here, naked,
writing this, bathed
in kitchen light and lavender
fragrance my wife
has told me is for peacefulness,
gratitude, and love.

Love Poem in Early May

–for Colleen

A weekend full of obligation
and the first summer rains, and we've
been distant and snarly with each other, my
wife and I, for days, both of us
feeling hemmed-in and diminished
by the necessary busyness of all we must accomplish
just to accomplish what's necessary, just to stay still.
And so this Sunday evening, our daughter
safely tucked into bed, our son
happily ensconced in a computer program,
we slip out for a little while, to ride our bikes
through the humid darkness, down to the park
by the bay, where once, on a night more dark
than tonight, I heard a manatee swim by,
breathing so heavily I thought I'd discovered
something—an old man on a secret journey, some sort
of endurance demonstration. I just stood there, blind
in the dark, listening, as the breathing grew steadily
distant, then vanished. But tonight the moon's bright enough
to light up the streets. We glide silently
along, breathing tree-sweat humidity and the perfumes
of a sub-tropic summer night: a whiff of what was here
before this place grew messy and too overwrought
to be anybody's home for long, or so
it sometimes seems. But the scent of night-blooming
jasmine, the smell of secret-dark-blossoming
cactus flowers opening stops us. We just breathe
until Colleen whispers something, taps my arm, and points,

and *there*, standing still as pure attention, tail
curled up and swept out and brushing the ground
at once, luxuriant and yet pricked to sharp awareness,
nose and oversized ears pointed toward us,
legs in mid stride, a fox is standing
right there in front of us, standing in our neighbor's yard,
in the false silence of purring air conditioners
and distant traffic, looking calmly at us,
darting a few steps, then stopping to stare at us
staring back at him, so thin, balanced perfectly
in silence. He doesn't seem at all afraid,
just *there*, so I lean my bike gently down
into the dewy grass to take a step toward him,
hand outstretched in false offering, as though I had food;
I step closer, whispering *I mean no harm*,
whispering *just let me get a better look at you, my friend...*

The Stories We Can Never Tell

We got up early to walk along the beach
which looked empty at first but was scattered with large fish
that had somehow been cast beyond the reach of waves
and were flapping a foot or more into the air,
landing with a thud on the wet sand.
We made a game of catching them in mid-air, tossing them
back into the waves, one after the other,
until they all were swimming again, and then
we walked, looking for shells and beach glass,
taking simple pleasure in our nearly naked bodies
in the sun and salt air: So when I mentioned
I believe the body and soul can know themselves
only together, that they are undefined
apart, I meant to imply something larger,
more inclusive, grounded and wild,
that reaches back into the stories we can never tell
because we are the arc of them, because we are their breathing.

The Point of Touching

One night, long after the children and I had fallen asleep, my wife
lit candles in every room of our house, took off her clothes, and went
outside, naked, to sketch charcoal impressions of the candle-glowing
house full of sleepers and light she loved. Then she took a scissors
and cut a lock of hair from each of us—me, our children, herself—and
buried our hair at the drip line of our gumbo-limbo tree. She played
her cello then, in our candle-lit living room, until dawn yawned at the
windows, and then she blew out the candles, came to bed, and slept
like a leaf flowing downstream, and slept like words in some forgotten
language. When she woke, at noon, there was no one home to talk to,
so she never told us anything—except in the way she touched me any-
where that evening, the way she kisses me some nights: with a yearn-
ing that makes me stop growing older for a few moments, reverses the
direction of my blood, yes, and makes me glow. And that's the point of
touching, isn't it? To make our bodies real? Things like that are some-
times closer than the world, closer than our words, closer even than our-
selves. So other nights I stay up beyond anyone, pacing the sidewalk
like the good husband I am, back and forth, back and forth—until I
finally wear away and vanish, like light itself, like life, or like fragrance
from the drowsy flowers growing butterflies and honey bees, growing
webs and brighter hues around our gumbo-limbo tree.

Night Animals

Small animals pulled out of our bodies
to sniff around our bedroom, into our closets,
into my wife's cello, which she'd laid on its side,
still humming, before turning out the light.

They chattered and sang and woke other animals
in the walls, to call to the creatures beneath
the house and those who live inside
the pipes and insulation.

Soon the whole house was singing and we were
breathing more deeply in sleep.

Sometimes I dream of floating where jellyfish
thicken the currents. I watch the way they move
as I float there, until I move like them.

My wife says she dreams I am tall, with sleek fur—
and what can I do but hug her?
Animals crawl across us, gnawing us in places

we'll never notice, though if we sleep
long enough together, we might grow grasses
and trees where there have only been wild
flowers and dragonflies, butterflies and bees,

none of which lives longer than a season.

The Same

blood that courses through fingers courses
through knee-skin and forehead, courses through brains
inside the brain, where we are not allowed,
where long-dead people we loved and never met
converse, by chemical reaction.
This morning my wife has placed a vase of flowers
on the dining room table. When I open the window,
a breeze disturbs their petals and a *deja-vu*
perfume takes me: I love her more
than I loved her twenty years ago.
So should I bow in gratitude
to flowers, to breeze? *Grace to be born...*
And what part does blood take in loving, in everyday
thinking, in feeling such gratitude we seem
our own harmonics? Certain moments I could feel
the blood move around my body, feel it
rush through the tiny branches and twigs
of the arteries, back into the veins that take it
back into the heart, which sends it back around again...

After Months of Careful Deliberation

my love has decided to take me apart.
She says I've been forgetting things lately, that she wants
to see me laid out on the floor so she can tell
what's broken and replace it. My love is good
with her hands; she loves to examine things closely,
to figure out by touching how the world works.
As a child in Colorado, she tied flies and caught the limit.
And she doesn't mind gutting things, cutting things, mending.
She's an expert with a map. When we drove cross country
in a VW bus, twenty years ago, she had to crawl
between the front tires and hold a connection
every time we started up. I turned the key.
That was the trip we drove to Northern Maine
to visit her old friend in his cabin in the woods.
Snow fell as we drove although it was only
October. That was the trip we got lost
in the woods in a blizzard, looking for this old friend
who knew about trees and the way water flows
underground for thousands of years before
we drink it, who'd taught her so many wonderful
facts about nature. And I just followed her,
yearning to see something wild, a moose
or even a bear, wondering where
this great friend was living, hoping we'd never find him.

Unplayed Music

Twenty years ago, newly married, my wife and I
paddled an aluminum canoe as far out
as nightfall, slipped into the cool water and floated
on our backs, guessing constellations, watching
for shooting stars. When a gust blew our boat
off into the darkness, we followed, listening
for the slap of waves against its metal hull, reassuring
each other: *It can't have blown too far.* But by the time
we finally caught it, we didn't have the strength
to climb back in, so we drifted into shore
on the tide, hanging from the gunwales, letting
most of our clothes drift away, admitting things
we tried to deny later, intimate
stories that might have changed everything. By the time
we reached shore, we were delirious. Without a word,
my naked wife pulled the canoe a few steps
into the water. She pushed. We watched it disappear
into the darkness, and then we walked home
through the empty streets, slipped between clean sheets
and slept all day inside each other
the way unplayed music
sleeps inside noise.

Distances

have shrunk, the guest lecturer informed us,
to half their former dimensions, in only
the past ten years or so, and so,

to keep things balanced, we must use different
instruments to measure things, and different concepts
of measurement, new tools—or time itself

may be thrown off kilter, and we may well find
we've already lived our entire lives,
we're already dead and buried!

Everyone nodded and pondered and took notes.
Someone raised a hand. I could hear birds
singing, even through the sealed window, and I

wished I could identify species by song,
and I wondered how many birds live here, how many
pass through this city on their bi-yearly

journeys, how many different kinds
of songs I'd have to memorize before
I could know them all by heart.

Behind Our Memories, Our Larger Families Wait

Our other father wanted to taste the milk
of every species of mammal in North America
because he believed our human race
started in milk, and because he loved breasts.

After that he hoped to make
a journey collecting eggs, not only
bird, but lizard, spider, insect
eggs as well, to taste them, moving

ever lower on the great chain until
he understood the diversity and subtle
textures of life on this continent with
knowledge he carried
on the tongue and in the blood.

He walked everywhere, and he slept outside
most nights. He believed that if he learned to focus
well enough he would eventually be able
to tell the size of a field with his eyes

shut, be able to smell what mammals
lived in a wood and how many different
species of tree lived there, too. He wanted
to fashion a language that incorporated barks

and purrings of all the wild creatures he encountered
so maybe a more nearly universal language
might be sung, at least in some
rudimentary form, and he tried to move

exactly like certain wild creatures, to make
only their sounds for days, to sleep
in the positions he'd observed them sleeping, to hide
the way they hid, to vanish the way

they vanished. Eventually he'd learn to fly,
to breathe under water, to live without thinking
as a human. And then he'd move on
to trees and flowers, on to wind and silence

*

As dusk fell, my children and I walked along the train tracks, through a
run-down neighborhood, across a black, shallow river in which mana-
tees lolled. We watched the wind breathe butterflies and tiny birds; we
watched a kingfisher shoot its hatchet body at its own shadow, skim the
water lightly, circle up and again. That night I dreamed I'd given birth
to a baby whose umbilical cord looked like a hairy arm. I dreamed
she dreamed of crawling back inside, and I yearned to let her go back
in; I breathed myself larger to make a space for her. And that kind of
breathing means something, sure, as smells mean something when we
haven't slept far enough inside ourselves and walk around all day like
a half-opened door. The fragrance of wild orange blows through our
house all night while we sleep, intoxicating memories.

I opened the back door one late night and walked out
and knew what it would feel like when I had at last to disappear.

*

A small dog lives inside a lonely man, in a little room
built into the intestines like a tree house in a tree.
At night while the man sleeps, the dog keeps faithful watch

in the absolute darkness; he barks at all suspicious
noises: the gurgle and grunt of digestion,
the moan, the cough, the rasp of troubled sleep.
Some nights the man is awakened by the barking
from deep inside his body, so he lets his dog out
to sniff his apartment, to show him all's well.
And the good dog never wants to go back inside
when the man smiles and whispers, raises his shirt
and pats his hairy belly—but he is just
a dog, after all, so he does what he is told.
He likes being in there when his master walks
through the city, singing softly, or talking to himself.
He's comforted by the lulling rhythms of the man's walk,
and he dreams, while he sits in that man-dark, of wolves
and foxes, vast fields he could run across
until he grew powerful and smart as pure hunger,
until he might swallow a human, keep him
inside his body, which is like a vast woods
before any stories we've ever heard were told,
before anybody had walked across the snow,
before there was *before*. And there he'd let his human free.

*

When doctors cut open this old man to fix his heart,
they found a tree, just behind the breast bone,
thick and leafy, tall, full of insects,
animals and birds.

And when they dug deeper, they found not just
the one tree, but a whole forest full of flowers,
rivers and animals they'd believed extremely rare,
even extinct. They discovered they could wander

into this forest, just by pulling back
the dead man's chest like a door, ducking,
and stepping in—

*

I read, half asleep in pre-dawn dark,
standing in the kitchen after making my children's lunches,

of a man who'd been arrested walking naked through the city
carrying a dress, who had tried to get dressed
when he saw the cops coming, an old man, almost
seventy. In fact he was Ernest Hemingway's
youngest son, who called himself Gloria
sometimes, whose real name was Gregory Hemingway,
a medical doctor who hadn't practiced
in years, who'd been married a number of times
and had seven children, who'd written several books
about his father—who was, according
to the police who arrested him, a *perfect gentleman*.
The next day, according to *The Herald*, he'd been found
dead in his cell—in the *women's* unit—.

Then I drove my daughter to school,
came home and walked around my garden inspecting
the papaya and the wild lime, the scrawny carambola,
the basil and the wilting banana trees.
I watched mourning doves knock seed from the feeder
to the ground, flutter down and eat, oblivious
to the neighbor's cat, crouched amateurishly
in the scrubby grass—.
The big trees were still dripping from last night's rain.

When a drop hit my head, I was surprised at how cold it felt,
reminded, as I so often am these days,
of how thin my hair has grown lately, how quickly
our bodies fall away from us, before we've used them
in all the ways we thought we would. I looked up and noticed

the tree was in flower: Small buds were opening,
spider webs were strung between the branches, they were filled
with drops of rain and the bodies of insects
whose insides had been sucked dry, who were almost as light
as air. *Someday I'll be as light as air*

I thought, without the usual regret. And then I headed off to work.

In Miami

Looking for a picture to help my daughter
with a school presentation, I open Jansen's
History of Art at random and find
a pressed flower, picked in Vermont twenty
years ago, when Colleen was pregnant,
the summer we started a gallery and swam
in the cold West River, behind a small corn field,
naked. I don't remember now

how we met our midwife; I can see us driving
a tunnel of trees, out to her small farm.
A bulky British woman with home-cut
hair and a twitch, she wore a nightgown-dress
and rubber boots as she talked sarcastically
about doctors—and people in general, belying
her *gentle gentle gentle* approach
to childbirth. The night our first child was born

and died, that midwife sat knitting calmly,
until it was too late: Suddenly the air
charged as she panicked, begged Colleen
to push harder, ordered me to lean
on my wife's belly, to ignore her screams.
When she cut Colleen, the baby gushed
out, limp and beautiful, perfectly
formed, already gone.

That winter I drove a bread truck town to town,
along back roads, through beautiful country.
We cross-country skied every day and we made
good friends, but we couldn't stay.

My daughter holds the dried flower
up into the light.

6

from
Stationary Wind (2004), and
Swimmer Dreams (2005)

Hunger

The young men who drive around aimlessly all night,
who stop at convenience stores to try to find romance,
who blast their radios as though anyone were listening
and might be impressed. The young men who sit
all night on bar stools growing their stubble;
the young men who live alone and hardly ever talk.
The deer who are starving, who walk through town
eating the paint on old windowsills, tufts
of grass that poke out through the cruddy gray snow,
who yearn for hunting season, who are chased by tattered dogs
down the plowed streets. The junk cars in the back yards;
the old men sitting deaf in front of loud TVs
scratching their balls, calling to their wives
who live just out of ear shot, taking care of everything;
the people on the TV talking on and on;
the hopeful young girls, putting on their makeup
carefully in silence, an hour before dawn.

Guitar

I built this guitar from our double bed
every morning before I dressed for work,
as darkness grained into light. I worked
outdoors: I loved the dew-soaked quiet
and the songs of the first birds. I tore that bed apart
slowly, remembering the nights my wife
and I had slept there hugging, and the nights
our small children filled the space between us,
when that bed was a raft we delighted to float
wherever the currents ran—
I thought if I built it carefully enough
my guitar might retain
the hum of that contentment.

The bed was a wedding gift. My grandmother told us
her grandfather had made it, from trees he'd cut
from his own land and milled with his bare hands.
She told us she thought she'd been conceived there.
She said her own daughter, my mother, had too,
as I had, and our children. It would make a good guitar.

Someday, I promised, I would learn to play
and prove to my family I hadn't been wasting
my life, ruining their most valuable possessions
for nothing. Someday I'd finish building
my instrument and sing so beautifully everyone
would understand. Until then, we'd sleep on the floor
and I'd sing *a cappella,* and I'd get up before
the birds, every morning, to whittle and nuance
dark wood in the dark, and wonder what possessed me.

Happiness

Or consider the bones in the tree that shades
a house full of children. The birds that lifted
those bones from the ground and picked them clean
are long gone now, to another tree.

Jawbone. Pelvis. Skullbone. Ribs.
Someone is singing inside the house.

I woke refreshed in an unfamiliar bedroom
where even the air was interesting, someone
was moving and singing just out of sight,
and I told myself once more: *This must be happiness.*

Flock and Shadow

> *... inevitably, a thing well suited to its surroundings—*
> *a snowflake, a sailing ship, or a spoon—acquires*
> *a true beauty of refinement: the soft dove-brown*
> *of the buff-breasted sandpiper, the sun color of*
> *the golden plover, the warm leaf tones of the*
> *woodcock are essences of earth and grass, of*
> *cloud shadow and the swift seasons.*
> —Peter Matthiessen, *The Wind Birds*

1.

Every bird at my feeder is someone I'd love
to sit with in a beautiful garden
beside the ocean—and who cares how much
wine we drink

      because afterwards we'll swim
until we are refreshed, and then we'll take a nap
in a cream-colored room with translucent curtains
and a quilted bed. Each bird at my feeder
is someone I've wanted

      to speak a foreign language with—
it doesn't matter which one—to decide we're going
to move away together

      to where that foreign tongue
is spoken, to leave without packing. *Goodbye.*
Each of these birds has been inside the house
of my body. *Come in.* Yes, the windows
are so clean there might as well be no glass
at all. As though there were no real world
beyond these small rooms. *Come closer.* Small birds
are singing between us as though the air
between us were different

from air in the rest
of the day, as though there were a waterfall of air
between us when we look at each other with just
the right expression. We are full of heavy bones,
but they hardly matter, since we are also full
of bird bones, which are hollow. And light.

2.

    (Whatever you feel becomes part of your nerves,
someone chatted over champagne, reaching out to touch me
gently on the wrist. We were standing outside
on damp grass. *What you hear becomes*
part of the ear, she said, *and the more*
deeply you listen the more fully the sound
becomes you. What you taste with pleasure
becomes your tongue. She smiled. I looked away.
There were moths in the grass. They fluttered up with each step
we took. Sometimes a cloud of moths
swirled up into the torches that burned
around the yard, sparked briefly,
then fell back to the grass. What I thought at first
was the smell of their burning was actually the scent
of perfumed bodies moving beneath
perfumed clothes and across a dark yard
in which rare flowers blossomed, sending out fragrances
to seduce what they needed from the night.)

3.
I read yesterday that by the middle
    of the next century, all the largest
predators but us
will be *functionally extinct.*

I read there is little anyone can do
about it, little to change the course
    of the world we've created as it works
on the world we have not. I read yesterday

of a man who'd had his eyesight restored
    after a lifetime of blindness, who couldn't
recognize anyone—the various colors
in his wife's hair confused and frightened him

a little. Where, I wondered, was the person
he'd touched before he could see? How did she
    look to him now, when they touched? And where
was he? I mean the person who'd been blind.

4.
And everywhere I seem to be, birds are singing just beyond
the window, barely audible above the hum of air
conditioner, TV, or traffic, singing
their intricate beautiful messages, like

parts of myself I often find
too easy to ignore. But as soon as I lean
close, turn off the machinery, hold
my breath and listen, they scatter, flying

off in a burst and a breath, leaving
silence to settle behind, reminding me
of the dreams I keep at the tip of my tongue,
of the songs I sing, just breathing.

Trees Filled With Hair

Then someone built a new kind of tree
that produced a new kind of fruit completely
unlike any other.
The fruit looked like some kind of skeleton.
We pulled the bones off to eat it.

That tree grew anywhere; that tree had leaves
that looked like eyelashes and seemed sometimes
to blink in the sun. That tree smelled like something
we'd loved once and lost and now had found again.

Birds that were new to our region began
to land in that tree and sing in voices
that sounded like babies crying in the night
and woke us. We wanted to get up and comfort them,
but they were only birds, and we were weary.

So we closed up the house, and we told each other stories
of who we'd been before, and who we'd been before that
and who we'd been before before, and so on through the night.

The Simple Truth

I met a man in the grocery store checkout line
who told me—out of the blue—he couldn't
recognize himself in the mirror, although
he felt perfectly normal otherwise—responsible,
reasonably content, married twenty years.
Each time he looked in the mirror, he told me
while I unloaded my groceries, he saw
a different person, and he had to touch
his cheeks or speak his own name aloud
while he stared at himself, to ascertain who was
staring back at him. He wanted me to know
how hard it was to shave. He wanted to explain
how, sometimes, when he looked at other men's faces,
he thought he saw his own features reflected back at him.
He told me he winked to test what he saw,
to see if that other face winked at the same time
or a moment later, in response. That could be
awkward, obviously. He said he thought he recognized me,
reached out and touched my face, standing there in line,
while the check-out woman scowled and the people lined up
behind us made noises of impatience with their carts.
I stared back hard as though I didn't know him,
but then I gave in, reached out and touched
his face in reassurance, and gazed into his eyes.

Only Child

My father dressed up as though he were my mother
who dressed up like me, who pretended I was her.
We spent a whole year as each other, to discover
who we really were. I still can't comprehend
how my mother's clothes fit me so well,
or how she, with her full figure, fit into my jeans.

My father wore makeup to understand our world.
Certain words, he said, are disguises, like love
and happiness; others wear jackets
woven of translucent wings, as though they could still fly.

I walked around as a middle-aged woman,
afraid some boy might see through my disguise
and tell the whole school. My mother pretended
she looked just like me, but no one was fooled
for long. Except my father. He kept whispering words
of passion into my disguise, asking me to dance.

Anything I Really Mean

There are so many butterflies, our windshield fogs
even when we're doing errands, and we have to pull over,
get out, and scrape their mucky bodies off

to be certain where we are. There's so much wing-dust
in the air, I mostly sneeze instead of saying
anything I really mean. But listen: Last night

we walked hand in hand to the river that runs
through the middle of our town, my wife and I.
We watched mica-colored fish rise to snatch yellow
butterflies from twilight. Smiling, my wife

took off her clothes and waded out into
the river, which spreads out into the bay—

She swayed her arms gently and the yellow butterflies
flew up around her. She called back to me
to join her. Dusk thickened around us.

I leaned on the railing and watched her wade deeper.
I watched her dive in and start her pale swimming.
Her clothes were folded neatly on the wall beside my feet.
I listened to her body splash out into the dark.

Aunt Betty

When Aunt Betty was little
she kept her dolls in a fish tank, a glass house
of flaxen-haired babies she nursed and groomed.

My mother keeps those dolls still
in a shoe box under her bed—
heavy, yellow, grim-faced—
in remembrance of happier days.

Her sister, she's told us, loved to give things away.
Sometimes she seemed to let go of herself,
stepped out of her coat like a shadow.
Once, after school, she gave away her favorite shoes
to a girl she'd just met, as a gesture of friendship—
a girl with bigger feet than she—
and walked barefoot in the snow across Brooklyn.

My mother loves to show us pictures of her sister,
who looks like a chair in some photos and a sofa
in others. In my mother's favorite portrait
Aunt Betty is a vase on the dining room table;
in another she's a small patch of scrubby city garden
and a row of heavy cars weighing down a winter avenue.

Bath

She told me a story about beehives and smoke.
She bathed me gently and explained how bees learned
to buzz, and why. She scrubbed my hair
and made up a story about bear cubs who ate
too much honey and fell asleep
so long they evolved into men, like I
would be someday. I lay back in the warm bath
and heard someone singing in the apartment next door.
I wanted just to lie there and listen to that singing
and to my mother's stories. The bathroom was steamy.
My brother was sleeping. Winter outside.
My mother took her clothes off, got into the bath
and asked me to wash her back; she lit a cigarette
and laid it on the edge of the bathtub while I washed her.
The smoke stung my eyes, so I ducked under the water
and opened them wide. The singing next door
was louder underwater. My mother was telling me
a story about the ocean, about mermaids who charmed
young sailors who'd been living at sea for years—
long enough, she said, to feel forgotten back home
where their sweethearts and wives had probably deserted them.
It was a long story. I washed my mother's back again
and again while she talked. And we stayed in that water
so long it grew cold. Eventually the singing
next door turned into the radio news.
Eventually my brother woke up and started crying
and my mother went to comfort him. The water was low
and cold without her body, so I turned on the hot
and lay back again. I knew it was already

dark outside, though the bathroom had no window.
I could feel that dark, somehow, in the sounds around me.

Several Ways to Vanish

One summer afternoon my girlfriend asked me
to tighten her belt so her waist would look smaller.

While she sucked her belly, I pulled tight and fastened.
And when she exhaled, her whole body, which was skinny
and frail, bulged around her tight belt.
When I reached out to unfasten the buckle, she batted
my hand away playfully: *You'll like me more.*

A family of foxes lived beneath her parents' house.
In the evening when we sat on the porch and held hands
they yapped and barked softly right beneath our feet.
One evening my girlfriend climbed through the crawl space
between the floor and the ground to try
to scare them away. She'd grown thinner every day.

I could hear her crawling below us while her father
talked about varnishes and waxes and different kinds
of oil, about lubricants and additives, sealants
and adhesives. He talked about plumbing supplies,
about deck stain and mildew. I watched fireflies
rise from the damp grass
into the star-filled sky.

Her mother brought out a plate of warm cookies.
My girlfriend knocked on the floor and called
for a flashlight. *Coming dear,* we sang back in unison,
chewing. Her mother poured another glass of milk.

Jubilee

For days I've felt off kilter—ever since, standing
on a stepladder, screwing in a light bulb while talking
on the phone with some credit card salesman, I got
shocked by the light socket. *Zap!* I felt the shiver
run down my arm, up my shoulder and neck,
through my head, out my mouth, into the phone,
and across many miles, to the poor slob who was just
trying to sell me some credit I'll probably
need, who yelped like a kicked dog as I was
thrown to the floor by the shock, unhurt
but knocked akimbo. The radio came on then,
like magic, in the *zap* of that electric charge,
with a report about a so-called dead zone, bigger
than the state of New Jersey, out in the Gulf of Mexico.
—Along the Gulf beaches, millions of fish,
fleeing that dead zone, have been swimming too close
to shore, leaping into fishing boats, trying
to hide inside bathing suits. Entire schools
have been stranded in tide pools at low tide: so many
fish for the taking, people have been filling
wheelbarrows, hitching trailers to their pick-ups
and packing them with fish, feasting, giving thanks
for Mother Nature's wondrous bounty, singing jubilee.

Another Life

And once, as a child, I was taken to an underground
spring, down dark stairs, to a cave lit dimly
by a string of bare light bulbs and a single hole
in the ceiling, way above, through which sunlight streamed.

When I took off my clothes, dove into that cold
water and swam out, colorless cave
minnows surrounded me, gently kissing
my legs and naked body,

and when an afternoon rain started falling
outside, a shower streamed through the ceiling hole,
straight down into the center of the pool,
which was otherwise still. I floated on my back

and let that shower fall on my face
while the colorless minnows kissed my body
and the adults who'd brought me waited patiently,
indistinct figures against the dark shore.

Planting the House

This man and his wife, happily married
for over thirty years, planted a garden
of herbs and berries and hummingbird flowers
down the middle of the mattress of their raft-size bed.

At night they slept amidst the vines and flowers
and let night creatures crawl across their bodies.
They let the garden spread; they wanted to see
whether it would cover their mattress and extend

to the floor, to the walls of their room, whether
birds might land there, whether they could attract
butterflies and bees. The husband put a bird feeder
in the tomato patch and a bird bath on the bench

at the foot of their bed. These old people whose children
had moved away, had married, had lives in distant cities
started making love again, started sleeping deeply,
started dreaming vividly and remembering their dreams—

so they decided to plant their entire house
in vegetables and flowers. Soon they'd be able
to harvest their dinners without leaving home.
The whole house was fragrant with love and blossoming.

When friends came to visit, they marveled at the old couple's
energetic happiness, but they couldn't see
the fountains or the swimming hole the wife had installed
where the bath used to be. Neither could their children

or even their grandchildren. The swimming hole reminded them
of an underground spring they'd swum in once
so long ago it almost seemed a dream—a cave

full of clear water full of colorless fish
that nibbled at their bodies—like kisses—as they swam out
to the center in the darkness that was lit by a single
hole in the ceiling, through which sunlight streamed.

Color Blind

So I can't know my blue mind. So what?
So I've never visited the house where he lives
with his wife and dogs, where I sometimes imagine him
dozing in his blue hammock, while the mutts sniff around
in the bushes or scratch their fleas and whine—

My green mind is smitten by every pretty woman
he sees, so he stays home and watches TV
to be safe, while my red mind wakes at all hours
and barks for no reason, annoying us all.

My yellow mind might be content to be a river
or a small forest pond, clean enough to drink.

What fun to swim naked in water that clear,
to dive to the bottom, where it's numbing cold,
and taste that purity! But what I really mean

is this: In the vast mind of purple that still
looks black to my colorblind eyes, my father
lay down some nights and told me a story
and fell asleep beside me. When my mother looked in
and saw us lying there, she leaned down, kissed us
and turned off the light. Then I'd hear her

playing loud records. I'd hear her singing songs
in languages she didn't know. I'd hear her making phone calls,
and I'd smell the rich aromas of her cooking, of her perfume.
I heard her drive away one night, forever.
But the next night she came in, lay down beside me
and slept, turning gray.

So I lay between my parents in that black-and-white room.
I lay between their dreaming like a color in the dark.

Several Kinds of Privacy

1.

The salt marsh whispered in the rising tide
and brisk wind of late fall, as afternoon
grained into dusk and then real dark before
day should have ended. Walking home from school,
I wanted to linger at the edge of that marsh
and listen for the small birds nesting in the matted grass
just beyond the tide. I loved the sound
of wind through the high-tide grasses. I loved
the funky salt and oil-smelling water, and although
I yearned to stay, to listen to the evening,
I turned and headed home, down the unlit street,
through the remnant woods, singing softly as I walked,

and opened the front door on my parents, who were dancing
to the song I'd been singing as I walked, who smiled
into each other's eyes with such quiet passion
they didn't notice me. They were dancing to their own
voices. In the kitchen, dinner had been served.
Steam rose from our plates. My sister sat reading.
Candles flickered. The whole house was silent
except for the shuffle of our parents' barefoot dance
and the soft grace of their singing.

2.

Another afternoon my parents were playing
hide-and-seek when I got home from school.
My father still wore his suit and tie;
my mother was disheveled. They giggled and waved
when they saw me, then continued running

from room to room, peering around corners
and hiding behind chairs. My brother and sister
were upstairs listening to music. I could smell
dinner cooking. In the front yard the life-sized
snowman we'd made with winter's first blizzard
still stood, half melted and filthy.
At some point both parents hid so well
we couldn't find them, though their cocktails stood
on the kitchen counter, just as they'd left them,
ice cubes melting into that amber light.

Solstice

Our children's mother and father met
on an empty subway whose lights went out
beneath the river between Brooklyn
and Manhattan. The car filled with the light
of fireflies, which flickered and bobbed
around them by the thousands, like constellations
in a billion-year time-lapse planetarium show.
She held out her hand—she, who'd never
been out of the city nor seen a firefly—
and grasped one and held it cupped in her small hands
so she could peer in.
He watched her carry it upstairs
and out into the evening, not yet dark,
this longest day of the year,
the first night of summer, and called out: *Wait*,
glowing with tenderness toward her, and held out
a small cardboard matchbook. *Keep it in this,*
for good luck. She smiled. *But then it won't live,*
she said, smiled brighter, and opened her hands.

White Birds

We called her Sweetpea, because she was so sweet
and because it made her smile. I don't know how old she was,
certainly near thirty though she was baby-fat plump,
and she always smiled shyly, like a little child.
She lived with her parents on the other side of Otter Creek
in a small house that abutted the marshes.
Whenever she saw us exploring the swamps
with our spears or walking sticks, throwing rocks and telling wild
stories, a few friends and my brother and me,
she'd run down to join us, always barefoot, even
in cold weather, even at high tide when the marsh grass
was almost underwater. And she'd always tell us something
interesting in some roundabout way.
She had long straight brown hair cut in bangs across
her forehead, and delicate hands.
She'd walk with us, talking quick streams of thought
that seemed unrelated unless you really listened,
in which case the connections between one thing
and the next made wonderful sense.
I wish I could remember what she told us about wind and tide.
I wish I could recall what she said about snow.

One afternoon, standing in the rushes,
barefoot as always, in water to her knees,
hem of her dress getting wet, looking up
into the white October sky,
she told us there were birds up there, too high
for us to see, flying by, going south.
Higher than the clouds, she said,
big birds, white. And they might even be singing.

She told us those birds always brought good news
wherever they landed. And then she called out
in a clear, high voice, in words no one had heard before,
as though to call those white birds down,
make them land here, make us lucky.
It was dusk. We stood still and listened to her singing
and listened to the water in the marsh suck and pull,
until a man crossed the road, an old man, and called her:
Mary Catherine he whispered to her gently;
darling Mary Catherine, come home, come home...

Yet Another Use for Poetry

I worked in the garden all afternoon,
cutting back the fox grape and fungus-withered myrtle leaves,
hacking brush away, pulling over-eager ferns
and shade-killed plantain trees. I filled the bird feeders
and watched butterflies trace their vague Cyrillic messages
as spider webs glistened in the sapodilla tree.
While I worked, our neighbors sprayed insecticide and weed control.
They blared classic rock. I dreamed idyllic privacy—
a coral-limestone trail through wild coffee, a bench
beneath our firebush tree, the peaceful
gurgle of a fountain, a reflecting pool. Or silence.

Our neighbors sang along to "Hot Blooded" and the Doobies.
When they cranked up their leaf blower, I went inside,
suddenly inspired, to gather certain books
by writers I love: *Cold Mountain* and *Gawain*,
Anonymous and *Ever After*—I pruned my library
a little, went back out and planted those authors
page by page along my garden wall:

Someday we'll have a cabin on a mountainside beneath
jackpine and cliff walls, looking out across
pristine wilderness; and someday we'll swim naked
in a vivid lake; we might paddle rivers
upstream, exhausted, with miles to go and darkness
rising from the current, and swallows gliding just above
our heads, dipping to skim the surface lightly
with their beaks and the tips of their delicate sharp wings—

Laughter

Next door, a woman laughs so loudly
her laughter bursts out the open window,
is blown into the sky by a brisk wind, all the way
to the bay, still laughing, where it startles a young man
sitting on a bench, looking out at the waves,
who walks to the railing and leans over it as though
he might jump in fully clothed, or as though he could watch
that laughter move out across the water, becoming
a figure swimming out there, moving quickly
out where the power boats surge.
This young man squints out at the swimmer, who looks,
he imagines, like someone he once knew
who swam great distances for pleasure, whose breath
while he swam sounded like laughter.

His wife is still asleep when he returns home.
We've been sleeping for years, he thinks, whispers
laughter into her ear, as he strokes
her hair and face. And that laughter moves down
tunnels and canals, through forests of sensitive
follicles, for miles, deep into her body,
until it reaches silence, where it becomes a kind of tree
whose leaves glisten brightly in the stationary wind

as she wakes, looks out the window, and hears
her husband laughing gently, and calling out her name.

Nurture

The trampoline our children used to jump on by the hour sits quietly beneath the huge avocado tree, which is full of lizards and birds, cactus and fungi, and—in this rainy season—small puddles in crotches and knotholes, where tiny wiggling creatures live. As the avocados ripen, squirrels nibble at their stems until the fruit falls, to crack open on the ground. Then the squirrels, raccoons and opossums feast, while we sleep behind closed windows in our air-conditioned dark. Some of the squirrel-picked avocados land on the trampoline, where they bounce around a few times as though they were alive and then lie still, un-bruised. Sometimes the girls next door, who speak only Spanish, climb over the wall between our houses, to jump and flip on the trampoline. I hear their jubilant laughter while I'm trying to read or write, ripe for any distraction. Unnoticed at the back door, I watch the girls jump. I watch the freshly-fallen avocados leap like small animals between them. Then I go out and say *hola* and ask them to be careful. I ask them if their mother knows where they are. I tell them I worry about broken bones and lawsuits. And childhood. They don't speak my language, but they smile beautifully. So I gather the heavy green fruit that bounces so high between them and makes them laugh so hard. I take it inside and put it in a brown paper bag to encourage it to ripen slowly, to stay firm and delicious as it mellows in that dark.

In Our Youth

Beauty without reasons, and without anxiety
over the lack of reasons: that may be what life
was like before we started making it up.
                              –Joan Acocella

We thought we might learn to capture the moment
with some new technology that combined
philosophy, syntax, and a way of moving
our bodies: a dream-time choreography.
We thought we might carry that moment like a smooth
stone in our pocket, a good luck charm
we could give someone else as a gift, someone
we cared about, someone we might just want
to fold ourselves into, someone we might want to
sleep with for years, in a room filled with artifacts
from our shared memories: masks of our courting,
flutes from our trance dances, shawls for the cold
above timber line, guidebooks and out-of-focus
snapshot self-portraits frozen in smiles
not exactly ever ours, ours forever now.

We hoped we might dream so vividly together
small nameless birds would fly from our bodies.
We held each other gently to watch those bright birds
disappear into the woods we loved to imagine,
as we talked of what we saw in there, back through the trees—
mushrooms, maybe orchids, mostly darkness. And we talked
nonsense or we sang, to flush out the birds,

to send them like moments of happiness swirling
up into the sky where they disappeared
until we learned to name them. Which never felt the same.

The Parents

One morning, my wife and I followed our eight-year-old
daughter along a crowded beach
just far enough behind her that she wasn't aware
we followed, as she walked with her energetic stride,
swinging her arms as though she were singing.

We marveled at her independence, at her
fearlessness; we compared her to other
children we knew, who would never have ventured
so far with such self-confidence.

We were congratulating ourselves on our excellent parenting
skills, laughing proudly at her spirit,
wondering where she was going with such
lively determination, when she stopped

and turned to look back: She was crying, with such
deep heaves she could hardly breathe, desperately
lost. She'd been frantically looking for us
and the place we'd left our towels—she feared
we'd forgotten her, gone home without her.

What could we say, kneeling beside her
in the bright sun—we'd been right there
the whole time, behind her, laughing affectionately
at the way she walked, as she walked

the wrong direction to find us, at the way
she looked from behind as she searched for us,
as she howled in such terror
we thought she was singing?

My Daughter's Birds

When my daughter plays her cello with the windows open, small birds land in the bushes and trees around our house and perch there, bobbing slightly up and down, singing softly in dissonant response. Mockingbirds stay a little further back, up in our gumbo limbo or sapodilla trees, learning as many of her songs as they can handle, flying off to sing cello music to other neighborhoods. When she was little she loved to hold my hand and walk with me. We'd sing nonsense songs to each other, improvising tunes and words until we got somewhere. Then we'd sit down in the grass to rest. Sometimes she fell asleep and I had to carry her. Once I carried her along an avenue of trees crowded with green parrots squawking down at us; another time we walked right up to blue heron standing in our neighbor's yard. And once the live oak in our back yard was filled with vultures, those timid birds of fearsome aspect, twenty or more, resting in the branches. We went out to look up at them, my daughter and I, but we didn't sing. Instead we did a dance, round and round, hopping up and down, hunching our shoulders, holding our arms straight out and floating ever higher on thermals, peacefully surveying the ground below, imagining our little selves watched over by dark birds, swooping down dramatically to see ourselves more clearly.

Still Life Toward Evening

The color of the fruit in the bowl on the kitchen table
when day turns dusky and your teenaged son
leans his head on his arms and almost falls asleep
while you move around, chopping
and mixing, listening to music
you've only lately discovered how to hear
without thinking about it. And you ask him how his day was—
fine. Just *fine?* You want to hear *wonderful.*
And you want him to tell you all his secrets, whom he loves—
and you want him to ask you for intimate advice—.
You love this music. He is almost dozing.
The apples and bananas on the table sing brightly.
Once you would have painted them; once you would have waited
until the light was just right; you would have put aside
everything and painted them. Then you would have wondered
what you couldn't capture that you needed, and why,
and you might have tried again, until the fruit was soft
with the character of dissolution, and then you might have cooked
a basic dinner, just because you had to eat.
And then you might have tried again, on into the evening.
Have some fruit you tell your son; *that will make you feel better,*
or stay just like that, so I can draw you sleeping...

Watching Other Animals

Animals first entered the imagination
as messengers and promises.
–John Berger

1.
Squirrels chatter, chewing through the stems
of our ripe avocados, to make the fruit fall
so they can feast, with the raccoons and opossums,
tonight, while we sleep. I am sitting outside
at dusk, waiting for my son to arrive home
from college—a short visit—listening to the *thuds*
of the falling avocados, drinking a glass
of wine, and reading in the fading light.

Today my wife and I sat on a sand bar
in the middle of the bay as the tide rose around us.
We talked, watching the ways the water
moved within itself as it glimmered
and reached, about the manatees we'd watched
the night before, who'd rolled together
for hours in slow-motion love, beside
the dock while a small crowd of humans gathered
to watch and marvel. We spoke of our son,
so happy. But gone. And then we paddled
back to the dock, where the manatees still lolled.

They raised their whiskered heads for a scratch,
snorted their funky breath in our faces,
inhaled, went under, and swam slowly away,
just below the surface, out where the speedboats
churn their loud propellers, and almost seem to fly.

2.

...and I thought of the fox my daughter and I saw
standing before overgrown ginger plants and wild cherry
        bushes, watching us, mud gray and almost

                invisible in the dusk of a day that had rained
        softly, that had just stopped raining and was now
misting into evening. We stood still, holding

        our breath; and then my daughter started moving
                slowly toward him; he barked at her, loudly,
        in a high-pitched, dark-grained voice, just once,

then faded into the bushes, as we
        returned to our bodies. My daughter was silent
                most of the walk home. Then she mentioned his calm

        balance—as though he were perfectly aware,
she said, of everything inside and outside
        the air. *I'd love to think they live*

                in our yard or under our house, that they go out
        at night to hunt while I'm falling asleep,
that they come home and curl up just as I wake...

3.

I've told this often: He was fifteen. We were riding bikes
at dusk, talking and watching each other
the way teenaged sons and their fathers do

when we came across a just-hatched, barely-moving bird
in the gutter. I thought we should just keep riding,
leave it there to die in peace: We had a meeting to get to

and the bird was so small it would never live anyway,
and it was just a bird, probably a pigeon, some weed-bird—

but before I could finish my sentence, my son
had dropped his new bike in the middle of the street,

had crouched down, held out cupped hands, and made
a soft noise I'd never heard before, until the bird
had pulled itself into his grasp.

We left our bikes behind and walked home, hopelessly
late for our meeting now. I helped him make a nest.

And all night my son woke himself every few hours
to feed that bird, to make sure it was as comfortable
as possible, to make certain it would live.

4.

    We loved walking at dusk in our humid clothes, tasting
fragrances: mango, night jasmine, afternoon
rain pooled in tannin-puddles in the crotches of our live oak,
where the tree frog tadpoles
swam in their thousand
identical selves, beginning to grow legs.

And we loved watching night birds fly into that tree
    without brushing a branch, perch there and start spearing
tadpole after tadpole from that summer-rain crotch-pond.

We loved walking through sticky spider webs cast across
the sidewalk since the night before, when we'd seen an owl
perched on the telephone wire: We'd sat down,
breathing with different lungs than usual,
we'd sat on the grass there beside the warm sidewalk
and watched—outside customary language—

until the owl leaped out—into its own outstretched, down-curved,
feather-fingered wings—and swung across a back yard

to his wife, my daughter sang. Indeed, toward a harmony
of owl voice in the dark—nothing like *whooo*—

a slate language: breath at the bottom of an old well,
wind in the space between our body and its atmosphere,
where microscopic hairs feel millimeter changes
and learn important news.

There were foxes in our neighborhood of closed-up, air-conditioned
houses, where the traffic never hushed. They hardly seemed
possible, though we saw them, though they lived beneath our rooms—

And often I wished I had the language to say
maybe we were foxes, to my children, in the way
I meant it. *Maybe we were owls once, or tadpoles. Listen*—

Where were we, my loves, before we came here?
Where are we now? And what kind of bee
pollinated night-blooming cactus flowers opening
to the moon we hardly noticed, rising through the avocado tree?

Caesura

Sometimes you must live as though you were grass
in a field of tall grass, as though you swayed
like the other grasses, and made the same soft
whisper they make; sometimes you must live

as though you were happy to be an insect or a tree,
as though you were a river, falling into rivers

falling into sea, as though you were a simple word.
Sometimes you must live as a pause inside a sentence,
as a speck of dark in a star-filled sky,
as a single breath. And then you blink your eyes...

I woke up in my bed on an ordinary morning
and knew I wasn't really there. Still, I lay there for awhile.
The radio was chattering, but it didn't make a sound
except inside my body, which was already gone.

The trees were full of ashes, that silent form of wind;
the wind was full of trees and grass it couldn't help collecting
as it tried to clutch itself into a solid body,
as it tried to speak. But there was nothing to be said.

Many of these poems originally appeared in the following books and chapbooks, most of them in limited editions.

Grateful acknowledgment is made to the publishers.

Looking Out: Moonsquilt Press, 1982
White Birds: M.A.F. Press, 1987
Lathe: Pygmy Forest Press, 1987
A Small Boat: University of Florida Press, 1990
Immaculate Bright Rooms: March Street Press, 1994
Many Simple Things: March Street Press, 1997
Sleeping With The Lights On: Pudding House Publications, 2000
Singing With My Father: March Street Press, 2001
Greatest Hits: Pudding House Publications, 2002
The Point of Touching: LeBow Publishing, 2002
Behind Our Memories: Adastra Press, 2003
Stationary Wind: March Street Press, 2004
Swimmer Dreams: Turning Point, 2005

Poems in the "New Poems" section have been published in the following journals: *The Comstock Review, Curbside Review, The Eleventh Muse, Harpur Palate, Hayden's Ferry Review, Iodine, Mi-Poesias, Parting Gifts, The Potomac Review, Rhino, The Tampa Review, The White Pelican Review.*

"Forgiveness" appeared in *Verse Daily*

I am grateful the Florida Division of Cultural Affairs for Individual Artist Fellowships.

Over the years, I have been blessed with generous and supportive friends, many of whom I rarely see, though they are often in my thoughts. Of these friends I would particularly like to thank: Bob and Susan Arnold, Shawn Beightol, Rick Campbell, Cindy Chinelly, Alan Davis, John Dufresne, Richard Jones, Mitchell Kaplan, Lyn and Jesse Millner, Karen Osborne, Burton Raffel, and Norma Watkins.

I would also like to thank Robert Bixby (March Street Press), John LeBow (John LeBow Books), and Gary Metras (Adastra Press) for their efforts on my behalf. I am immensely grateful.

Photo by: Colleen Hettich

Michael Hettich was born in New York City, and grew up in the city and its suburbs. He has lived in upstate New York, Colorado, North Florida, Vermont, and Miami, Florida, where he now lives with his family. Author of twelve previous books and chapbooks, his work has appeared widely in journals, among them *Witness, New Letters, TriQuarterly, Smartish Pace, Poetry East,* and *The Literary Review.* His awards include two Florida Individual Artist Fellowships, The Tales Prize (for *Swimmer Dreams*), and an Endowed Teaching Chair from Miami Dade College, where he teaches English and Creative Writing.